SWINBURNE

from a water-colour of 1862 by D. G. ROSSETTI,
in the Fitzwilliam Museum, Cambridge.

SWINBURNE

by

IAN FLETCHER

PUBLISHED FOR
THE BRITISH COUNCIL
BY LONGMAN GROUP LTD

LONGMAN GROUP LTD
Longman House, Burnt Mill, Harlow, Essex

*Associated companies, branches and
representatives throughout the world*

First published 1973

© Ian Fletcher 1973

*Printed in Great Britain by
F. Mildner & Sons, London, EC1R 5EJ*

ISBN 0 582 01228 7

ALGERNON CHARLES SWINBURNE

I

SWINBURNE is not a Victorian curiosity, but a highly original poet, an exhilarating metrist; his poetry explores unusual areas of experience and his lyricism, at its best, is rich and haunting. Yet till very lately he was a notorious critical 'case', a synonym almost for a literary disease. In his own lifetime a German journalist could place him definitively as a 'higher degenerate', one of the symptoms being the poet's love of repetition, 'echolalia'.

And if Swinburne's later fortunes were singular, so was his contemporary reception. His first volume was virtually ignored; his second made him famous; his third was attacked on all sides and the publisher cowed into withdrawing it. *Poems and Ballads* (1866) had violated that high Victorian decorum, the tacit assumption that poetry represented an extension of ethics by other means, its subject matter only what was well above the girdle. Swinburne's earlier lyrics are a breviary of Freudian insights. He gives voice to the dark underside of the Victorian psyche, writing of the aggressive, the cruel, even the demonic aspects of sexual love, and of the suppression or perversion of human instincts by social and religious tyrannies. And in *Atalanta in Calydon* (1865), that great dramatic poem, he arrives at the notion of 'the death of the family'; the contention that this institution is by nature oppressive and must be superseded by more flexible social forms. Swinburne surely intended to shock his public by anti-Christian gestures and erotic polemics; although such were certainly not the limits of his aims, yet his own *succès de scandale* engulfed him. Readers were dazzled or repulsed by the violent rhythms or topics of his verse.

Swinburne has also suffered from the familiar slump of reputation in the years succeeding an author's death—the fate of Shaw offers an obvious parallel. And before his fortunes could recover he became involved in the diffused attack of the 1920s on Victorianism in general. They were further soured by the critical propaganda for an autonomous 'modern' movement in poetry which was conducted largely by the 'modern' poets themselves. T. S. Eliot and Ezra Pound, for example, were understandably anxious to secure themselves an audience and that meant displacing their immediate predecessors. As Harold Bloom puts it, the poet *creates* his predecessors (by constructing fictions of literary history), but 'the relation of . . . the new poet to his predecessors cannot be cleansed of polemics or rivalry', and this rivalry stems from anxiety about poetic identity.

Such a strategy was intended to mask the fact that Eliot was himself a deeply romantic poet, and to suggest that his poetry had more in common with the seventeenth-century metaphysical poets, with their wit and word-play, than with the allegedly decaying romanticism of the late nineteenth century (the French, Baudelaire and the Symbolists, were absolvable). This involved the creation of a canon: Eliot called it 'the main stream'. Eliot was to describe his early essays as 'a by-product of my private poetry-workshop; or a prolongation of the thinking that went on to the formation of my own verse' and this late candour sanctioned the admission of some of the poets who had been formerly excluded from the 'main stream'. In America a race of literary journalists and 'new', close-reading and not infrequently neo-Christian critics arose, and since it had already been agreed that word-play, complexity and ambiguity were not to be found in Swinburne, he was largely absent from their searching analyses. In this country, Professor Leavis and his adepts had their version of literary history. The one great poet of the later Victorian period, greater than Tennyson or Browning, was Gerard Manley Hopkins, and had not Hopkins himself with the clairvoyance of genius said the last but one word on Swinburne: 'a perfect style must be of its age. In virtue of this archaism and on other grounds [Swinburne] must rank with the medievalists', and did not Swinburne suffer also from the defect of having 'no real understanding of rhythm'? Paradoxically Hopkins and Swinburne now appear as the most extreme of the Victorian poets, though extreme in radically different ways. But by a further paradox, Hopkins's response to the 'pied' particularity of things extends that stroking in of details so frequent in Tennyson, Browning and Rossetti. Hopkins is, indeed, as one critic has suggested, more Victorian than the Victorians in his inspired clutter of detail. Swinburne, however, moves towards music and Symbolist dream in attempting to create a closed world, without objects, through language. This point was made in Eliot's casuistical defence of Swinburne:

The poetry [of *Poems and Ballads*] is not morbid, it is not erotic, it is not destructive. These are adjectives which can be applied to the material, the human feelings, which in Swinburne's case do not exist. The morbidity is not of human feeling but of language. Language in a healthy state presents the object, is so close to the object that the two are identified.

For Eliot, Swinburne's verse is *sui generis*. But his description does not take account of its characteristic tension between *subject-matter* and *surface* which is the outcome of a moral horror different in quality but not in kind from that of Baudelaire, nor does it admit that word-play and complexity are to be encountered in Swinburne.

The comparison with Baudelaire is crucial, because of the French poet's influence. There are affinities: Woman as emblem of the unattainable; the 'quarrel with God'; the inversions of *Les Litanies de Satan* recalling a common use of litanies of supplication, worship and terror in contexts of disgust and revolt; there is a shared distrust of overt morality as falsifying experience, a shared awareness of ennui as the human condition. The distinctions, though, are sharp. Unlike Swinburne, Baudelaire possessed a gift for luminous concision and his ennui is counterpointed by an energy that is by no means always frenetic. Baudelaire is also more aware of the tang and resonance of objects and this enables him to correlate outer and inner landscapes. This particularly enriches his interpretations of the modern city with its workmen, prostitutes, and the number of lives momentarily and obliquely touching his consciousness. Wordsworth had presented London as an infernal carnival in the sixth book of *The Prelude*. Baudelaire's Paris is infernal also, but Wordsworth's healing image of the Blind Beggar is replaced by the procession of Seven Old Men through the dirty fog, who mysteriously embody the intimate nightmare of the outer world. To this nothing in Swinburne corresponds. If on one occasion at least he evokes an industrial landscape,[1] the human figures evade him.

There is, of course, an indictment for his admirers to answer. If Swinburne radiates some of the signs of genius—energy, abundance and a powerful literary identity—his range of subject seems slender. The metrical effects, surprising, stunning even at first, gradually dull the response by reliance on anapaests and iambs; the initial effect of wildness is eventually tamed by patterns of expectation; unlike Baudelaire, Swinburne did not dislocate his metres, while his alliterations were continuous, brash and self-indulgent. The poet has a harem of words to which he remains depressingly faithful: his vocabulary is often heavily Biblical with a manneristic profusion of God, Hell, serpents, stings, rods, flames and thunders, etc., a surprising characteristic in one who was so determinedly a hammer of the Christians. Swinburne's muse is indeed a kind of inverted Balaam: he curses God in the tones of an Old Testament prophet out of a job, or one perhaps resisting the

---

[1] . . .   Such nights as these in England, the small town
      Chatters and scrawls its purpose out in brown,
      Searing with steam the hill's dead naked shape;
      By juts of hurt impatience let's escape
      Quick sighs of fire from chimnied engine-works.
                          (*Unpublished fragment*)

burdens of office. And the subjects of Swinburne's verse
seem to melt into one subject. Whether he is exploring a
pungent sado-masochistic psychology or the sea as Mother
figure; or the liberation of Italy as emblem of man's
liberation from all tyrannies, religious or political; or
sounding the bracing moral suasions of the Navy League,
it makes little difference. The noxious rhythms, the vocabulary, blurred and generalized, persist, so that we can barely
tell if we are meant to admire a battleship or a breast.
Housman, one of Swinburne's best and wittiest critics sums
it up: 'The sea, like babies and liberty went into the sausage
machine into which he crammed anything and everything,
round goes the handle and out of the other end comes . . .
noise.' Housman admired some of the poems, but 'there is
no reason why they should begin where they do or end
where they do; there is no reason why the middle should
be in the middle; there is hardly a reason why, having once
begun, they should ever end at all; and it would be possible
to rearrange the stanzas which compose them in several
different orders without lessening their coherency or
impairing their effect.' But Tennyson's comment has an
equal aptness: 'He is a reed through which all things blow
into music.'

The most serious charge against Swinburne is that his
insights seem always to move towards the peripheral, the
immature. His work resounds with echoes from his wide
reading. Besides the Bible, there are the Classics, Jacobean
drama, the Continental literatures, the Border Ballads.
And literature fashioned out of other literature is finite.
Swinburne was sometimes a deliberate, often highly
accomplished pasticheur; he was also a clever parodist. His
pastiche and his parody can be readily enjoyed, but what of
involuntary parody? Too often, the poetry he proffers as
original reads like self-parody or self-echo. In displaying
such 'Alexandrian' symptoms, he is not, of course, alone.
Much Victorian poetry is self-consciously literary, abstracted
even from the more formalized gestures of Victorian

communication. But there is no poet whose style is so deliberate a literary mosaic. Even when Swinburne seems to speak most directly and feelingly to his reader, as in this passage from 'The Triumph of Time', he feels in quotation marks:

> 'What should such fellows as I do?' Nay,
> My Part were worse if I chose to play;
> For the worst is this after all; if they knew me,
> Not a soul on earth would pity me.

Understanding of one's state, incidentally, and acceptance of humiliation, should not be confused with self-pity.

II

Swinburne is one of our relatively few upper-class poets. His father, younger son of Sir John Swinburne (the baronetcy went back to 1660), was to achieve the rank of Admiral in the British Navy; his mother was the fourth daughter of the third Earl of Ashburnham. A cousin vividly describes Algernon's first appearance at Eton.

He stood there between his father and mother, with his wondering eyes fixed upon me! Under his arm he hugged his Bowdler's Shakespeare, a very precious treasure, bound in brown leather . . . He was strangely tiny. His limbs were small and delicate; and his sloping shoulders looked far too weak to carry his great head, the size of which was exaggerated by the tousled mass of red hair standing almost at right angles to it.

His actual size seems to have been about five feet. The cousin softens this description by alluding to Swinburne's voice as 'exquisitely soft . . . with a rather sing-song intonation', evidently the vatic, Romantic reading voice, which was common to Wordsworth (according to Tom Moore's journal), to Tennyson and to Yeats—as the last two have been preserved on record. Other accounts speak of his voice rising to an eldritch shrillness, of his dancing steps and continuous vivid movements.

Swinburne's bohemianism, republicanism and war with God, can be viewed as a patrician individualism. This would have seemed less odd two generations earlier, in the Regency period. It was mid-Victorian middle-class evangelical values which intensified its provocative qualities. Swinburne located (like Yeats) some of his most deeply felt values under the aristocratic notions of courage, honour and chivalry. Of his own courage, moral and physical, there can be no doubt: fearless on a horse, he was a passionate swimmer in dangerous seas. Undoubtedly, his small size led to a compensatory need to prove himself 'manly'— hence his stoical endurance of beatings at Eton, his drinking with the bunch, and his close association with vigorous male personalities.

Much of Swinburne's childhood was spent in the Isle of Wight and at his grandfather's family seat, Capheaton, in Northumberland, a county on the Scots borders. Northumberland's bleak spaces, its wildness in sea and wind, legends and traditional ballads strongly attracted him. Of these last, Swinburne made many imitations, capturing directness, dialect, brutality and anonymous narrative qualities with assured skill. The softer landscapes of the Isle of Wight passed also into his work. Close to the Swinburne house on that island lived his mother's sister Lady Mary Gordon and her husband Sir Henry, the Admiral's first cousin. Their daughter Mary Gordon, a tomboyish girl (like Swinburne she rode well), with some gift for literature, was the close companion of his earlier years, probably the central personality in his emotional life, and certainly a muse-figure. The two were so closely interrelated that marriage would have been considered dangerous and Swinburne's physical oddity must have constituted a warning eugenic emblem.

Algernon's wide and intense reading had been initiated by acquiring French and Italian from his mother, but he also read enthusiastically in his grandfather's large library at Capheaton which contained many French works. His education continued at Eton, to which he was sent in 1849 at the age of twelve. He seems to have become difficult, and after four years left school for three years of private tutoring, going up to Jowett's Balliol College, Oxford, in the year 1856. Swinburne was soon involved with a Club called Old Mortality, whose later members were to include Walter Pater and J. A. Symonds.

In 1857 he encountered the manic exuberance of Rossetti, Morris and Burne-Jones, who were busy with mural painting at the Oxford Union Debating Hall. The meeting was decisive in several ways. It confirmed Swinburne's devotion to literature and art. The imagery of the murals was Arthurian, and Swinburne was soon composing Arthurian verse in the naïve idiom of William Morris's *The Defence of Guenevere* (1858). Like numerous under-graduate groups, Old Mortality then proceeded to a magazine, *Undergraduate Papers*, to which Swinburne with characteristic versatility contributed poetry, an essay on his favourite Elizabethan and Jacobean dramatists, and an amusing mock-review. Jowett, who liked his young men to get along (and on) in the world, tended to disapprove of Swinburne's dedication to poetry. In 1858 and 1859, Swinburne was busy with writing and revising his *Rosamond*, a distinctly Pre-Raphaelite closet play, achieving a second class in Moderations, working at a prize poem on the life and death of Sir John Franklin, and experimenting with devout pastiches of Beaumont and Fletcher, full of their witty sexual perversities as well as his own flagellant fantasias. *Laugh and Lie Down* (1859) plays with the theme of homosexuality and this was to be repeated in later work. Swinburne's sexual life has been much discussed, the conclu-sions veering between sado-masochism and homosexuality. Discounting natural tendencies to the homoerotic, latent or displayed in many men, one must distinguish that, to quote Matthew Arnold, from any 'descent to the realm of immediate practice'. Possibly Swinburne had a playful relationship of this order with Simeon Solomon

(whose tastes were unequivocal), and he was undoubtedly
attracted to physically strong men. He was fascinated by
Watts Dunton's seven-year-old nephew in later life and on
happier terms with his mother than with his father. His
known relationships with women were both inconclusive.

With Jowett, Swinburne's later relationship was affec-
tionate enough, but it is probable that the Master was
involved in Swinburne's departure from Oxford in November 1860. The publication of two plays, *The Queen-Mother*
and *Rosamond*, may have confirmed Jowett's dubieties. In
the following year, Swinburne met a more dangerous
mentor: Richard Monckton Milnes, politician, man about
town, dim poet and collector of erotica. It was Milnes who
introduced to Swinburne another of his formative influences,
the Marquis de Sade. In 1862, Swinburne published poetry
and criticism in *The Spectator*, including his pioneering
article on Baudelaire. In London, he acquired a reputation
as a delphic talker, a genius, while to an American observer
he appeared as 'a tropical bird, high-crested, long-beaked,
quick-moving, with rapid utterance and screams of humour,
quite unlike any English lark or nightingale'. For a time he
joined Rossetti in that bizarre *ménage* at 16 Cheyne Walk,
with its menagerie and artists' models. The mythologizing
of Rossetti and his associates was already beginning, but
the story of Solomon and Swinburne sliding naked down
the banisters and Rossetti roaring at them for disturbing
his painting, has at least a typical truth. Rossetti's relationship to Swinburne was partly that of master to disciple and
they shared memories of Rossetti's wife Lizzie, who had
committed suicide in 1862, and to whom Swinburne had
been chivalrously devoted. In a friendly way, however,
Rossetti soon indicated that he wished to terminate the
co-tenancy.

Between 1862 and 1865 Swinburne was perfecting *Poems
and Ballads*. His main models were the metres of Greek
poetry, Shelley, Baudelaire, Blake, and a discovery which
he probably owed to Rossetti and which he greeted with the

same levity and admiration accorded to the 'divine' Marquis. This was the doctor from Georgia in the American 'old south', Thomas Holly Chivers, transcendentalist, and friend of Edgar Allan Poe, from whose poems those of Chivers are sometimes indistinguishable. Chivers's headlong metres are to be found in volumes of strange title such as *Eonchs of Ruby* and *Nacochee*. Very close to the note almost of burlesque in Swinburne's 'Dolores':

> Cold eyelids that hide like a jewel
>   Hard eyes that grow soft for an hour;
> The heavy white limbs, and the cruel
>   Red mouth like a venomous flower

is this from Chivers's 'Lily Adare':

> Her eyes, lily-lidded were azure,
>   Cerulean, celestial, divine—
> Suffused with the soul-light of pleasure,
>   Which drew all the soul out of mine,

even if Swinburne could barely emulate those languid rhyming vowels of the Southern States.

In 1863, Swinburne completed *Chastelard*, the first part of a trilogy devoted to his admired Mary Stuart, though the play was not to be published for another two years. In the autumn of that year he was staying with the Gordons on the Isle of Wight, helping Mary write her *Children of the Chapel*, a romance full of flagellation scenes, and at work on his masterpiece *Atalanta in Calydon*. From the same year dates what is probably the finest of his lyrical pieces 'The Triumph of Time'. It was now perhaps that Swinburne realized there was to be no intimate future with Mary, that he was condemned to being, as he put it in the words of Mary Stuart's rival, Elizabeth, 'but barren stock'. Mary Gordon was married two years later to a middle-aged military man, who lived in the north of Scotland. There was no meeting, and no surviving letters for another twenty-five years. Already Swinburne had begun his brilliant study of Blake, concluded a version of his novel *Love's Cross Currents*, and proceeded some way with another novel *Lesbia Brandon*, but he had also begun to drink excessively.

Of *The Queen-Mother* and *Rosamond* two notices only have been traced, both unfavourable; but with the publication of *Atalanta in Calydon* in 1865, Swinburne achieved immediate fame. Milnes is supposed to have engineered a programme for publicizing the book, made more attractive by Rossetti's subtle and original binding with its assymetrical Celtic and Greek decorative forms. The following year, Swinburne published *Poems and Ballads* (the contents of which were mostly earlier than *Atalanta*). One or two reviewers defended Swinburne's outspokenness but even John Morley, later a friend, who was free from the familiar Victorian notion that art should idealize the actual to promote public and domestic pieties, described the poet as 'the libidinous laureate of a pack of satyrs' and complained, 'is there nothing in woman worth singing about except "quivering flanks" . . . "splendid supple thighs" ... "stinging and biting"?' Rossetti, concerned that Swinburne was without normal sexual experience with women, paid Adah Isaacs Menken, burly busty circus-rider and writer of Whitmanesque verse, the sum of ten pounds to seduce the poet. Menken was honest enough to return the money with a complaint that echoed Morley's: 'I can't make him understand that biting's no use.' However, a change of direction in Swinburne's art, if not in his life, soon occurred. Early in 1867, Swinburne had completed a longish political poem, *A Song of Italy*, and in that same year he had written his 'Ode on the Insurrection at Candia'. In the following year he published 'Siena', one of those poems that were to form his volume on the liberation of Italy, *Songs before Sunrise*. An amusing, probably apocryphal story, told by Edmund Gosse, relates how a meeting of Swinburne's friends and associates including Jowett, Karl

Blind and Mazzini, was convened to discuss 'what could be done *with* and *for* Algernon'. That there were meetings of family and friends, we need not doubt. Swinburne was prepared to transfer his devotions to a lady as exacting, but nobler than Dolores, Our Lady of Pain. Or, as Edward Thomas puts it, 'Freedom or Liberty was a safer object of worship than Man, because she could never be embodied, though too easily personified'. Embodied, however, in the person of Mazzini, she was.

In 1868 appeared *William Blake* his greatest work in prose, in 1871 *Songs before Sunrise*, and in 1874 his 'double-length chronicle play' *Bothwell*: 1876 saw his second essay in Greek tragic poetry *Erechtheus* and 1878 the second series of *Poems and Ballads*, which comprised such cardinal pieces as his elegy on Baudelaire, 'Ave atque Vale' and 'The Forsaken Garden'. The last two were of all Swinburne's volumes the most indulgently reviewed.

Yet now, if we except *Tristram of Lyonesse* published in 1882, but begun early in the 1870s, a dozen or so poems and some criticism, his good work was finished, though he was to live for a further thirty-one years. In the 1870s, the alcoholic collapses became more frequent. After each crisis, Swinburne would rapidly recover in the family home, but on returning to his London rooms the cycle of crisis, collapse and recovery would recommence. He was becoming lonely. The most serious separation was from Rossetti, whose feelings of guilt followed by his unhappy affair with Jane Morris and the attacks on the fleshliness of his poetry, had finally brought him to attempted suicide. Rossetti's brother advised Swinburne not to approach his old friend and mentor. From 1872 to the time of Rossetti's death in April 1882, there was neither direct communication nor meeting. Increasingly Swinburne became dependent on the last of his father-figures, Theodore Watts (later Watts-Dunton), a solicitor with literary interests, who already had been usefully involved with Rossetti's affairs. In 1879, Watts was sanctioned by the Swinburne family

to take Algernon into care : the poet was by then forty-two
and for the next thirty years Watts acted as his guardian.
Points can be made against Watts: he was probably jealous
of Swinburne's old associates and tended to treat the poet
as his own property. Swinburne clearly became dependent
on him and made no attempt to break out of the suburban
prison at The Pines, 2 Putney Hill. Watts also influenced
Swinburne in the direction of conformism. The poet's
moral tone improved; he foamed at Parnell when in
earlier days he had pleaded for the Fenians; sonorously
slanged the Boers and rhapsodized over the Jubilee of the
Divine Victoria. Extravagantly loyal to friends, he had
however exhibited moral inflexibility even before The
Pines closed round him: in 1873, for example, when
Simeon Solomon had been charged with an act of homosexual indecency Swinburne's reaction had been one of
panic-stricken prudery.

Each morning, Swinburne would take a long healthy
walk across Putney to the Rose and Crown public house at
Wimbledon, South West London, for his single bottle of
beer, conducting a private baby show of his own on the
outward and return journeys. Indoors, on occasions of
celebration, a little wine might be drunk: if the demon
poetry had been domesticated, the demon drink had been
tamed. Increasing deafness cut off Swinburne still more
radically from the outer world, perhaps in the end even
from the other inhabitants of The Pines. Inwardly, he
seems to have been happy; his old friends he may have
lost; he had his books. In the April of 1909, there came
first influenza, then pneumonia, then death.

III

In 1876, when a new edition of *Poems and Ballads* was
proposed, their author suggested to his publishers that some
poems might be transferred to a volume of earlier work,

including also *The Queen-Mother, Rosamond* and various unpublished poems. His proposal, which was not taken up, would have clarified the central themes and tones of *Poems and Ballads*.

That earlier work mostly betrayed Pre-Raphaelite influence: Morris's juxtaposition of dream and violence, in Pater's phrase 'the desire of beauty quickened by the sense of death', and, more importantly, Rossetti's juxtaposition of realism and the supernatural. Rossetti, Jerome J. McGann has convincingly argued, deliberately manipulates Christian imagery in such a way as to exclude traditional responses. By emptying such imagery of its inherited content, Rossetti enables us to experience physical detail 'in a new and wholly sensational way', and this relates to his belief in Eros rather than Agape, that is in sexual affection exalted as the highest known value (though arguably Rossetti's final position involves, like Swinburne's, the sublimation of the self through art). In Rossetti's poem 'The Woodspurge', perfect grief leaves the speaker simply with the irreducible: 'The woodspurge has a cup of three.' It reads like a failed emblem in the tradition of the seventeenth-century poem of meditation, in which all natural objects lead the mind to a Creator who is also immanent within creation. But here the flower is no easy symbol of Trinitarian hope; what remains to the speaker is the 'the enormous relevance of the flower's non-symbolic fact. At that time and in that place the speaker gained a measure of relief from the simple act of observation . . . the poem hints at the mystery . . . in the mere fact of sensory observation.' If we compare Rossetti's 'The Woodspurge' with Swinburne's 'Sundew' we may perceive some distinction between the two poets. Swinburne's poem opens:

> A little marsh-plant, yellow green,
> And pricked at lip with tender red.
> Tread close, and either way you tread
> Some faint black water jets between
> Lest you should bruise the curious head.

and ends by rejecting the flower because it does not recall
the woman whom the speaker loves. The Sundew is
actually carnivorous, its tentacles extended in a rosette of
leaves. The appearance of precision here misleads and there
is no triumphant conclusion in the sufficiency of sensuous
experience. Rossetti's attitude to the Christian associations
he undercuts is in general decorous; similarly, Swinburne
in 'A Christmas Carol', suggested by one of Rossetti's
drawings, captures all the solemn candour of the form.
'The Two Knights', an early poem omitted from *Poems
and Ballads*, altogether capitulates to 'The Blessed Damozel',
but 'The Leper' interestingly marks the transition to
Swinburne's personal style. This dramatic lyric, somewhat
reminiscent of Morris's early manner, is spoken by a
medieval clerk whose love has a masochistic tinge. He
panders for the girl he hopelessly loves by bringing the
knight she desires to her bedroom in secret. She thanks her
'sweet friend' for preserving her from scandal. Then she
becomes afflicted with leprosy. All, including

> . . . he inside whose grasp all night
>   Her fervent body leapt or lay,
> Stained with sharp kisses red and white,
>   Found her a plague to spurn away.

The clerk hides her in a 'wattled' house and tends her:

> Six months, and I sit still and hold
>   In two cold palms her cold two feet.
> Her hair, half grey half ruined gold,
>   Thrills me and burns me in kissing it.
>
> Love bites and stings me through, to see
>   Her keen face made of sunken bones.
> Her worn-off eyelids madden me,
>   That were shot through with purple once.

Baudelaire's 'La Charogne' is a source, though the tone is
distinct. 'The Leper' ends with a moral casuistry that echoes

Browning's 'Porphyria's Lover'.

>It may be now she hath in sight
>Some better knowledge; still there clings
>The old question. Will not God do right?

The subdued metaphor throughout is 'the body of love':
communion. The speaker searching still for total communion,
emphasizes happily: he is necrophiliac, sacrilegious, vampir-
istic. The girl has been reduced to a *thing*.

Swinburne tops up the poem with a mock-source for this
fictive tale in his best Renaissance French. Identity begins
to be established here by parody and caricature, stylistic
and iconographical, used by the poet to transcend his source:
the hair, profuse sexual symbol among the Pre-Raphaelites,
is not 'dim' merely, as it becomes in Morris's 'Old Love', but
rancid, 'half grey half ruined gold', while pre-Raphaelite
archaism is also mocked. Through such ironic mockery of
his sources, Swinburne, like Donne, protects his tone from
absurdity or bathos.

IV

Those early poems were probably written before the
'moment of truth' between Swinburne and Mary Gordon;
the cousins' situation certainly underlay the remainder.
Mary and Algernon had shared a private world; part of
their mythology was Mary's fictional role as Swinburne's
younger brother at school, sympathetically involved in his
experiences of flogging. The relationship was so independent
of sexual distinction that the shock was more profound
when it became apparent they must separate; Mary must
marry. For this 'fall' from a world of unity, the family was
directly responsible and behind the family, Society, and the
power, 'God', which both expressed. This power, sensed
only as cruelty and violation, had been responsible for the
peculiarities of Swinburne's personality (and physique).

In his analysis of *Poems and Ballads*, Professor Morse Peckham distinguishes between 'self' and 'personality', which 'is simply something that is given . . . is, in a strange but true sense, entirely alien to oneself,' and in Swinburne's case, with the capacity to humiliate the self. Personality is Hell and can only be understood and accommodated to as far as possible. Swinburne's insights into his own psychology and his need to æstheticize the self, a transformation of concrete situation into artifice, result in peculiarities of style and negation of development. As Professor Peckham puts it: 'from the meaningless chaos of experiences, the self creates through art a world of order and value. Style offers a stance, an orientation, safely to experience that chaos . . . the selfhood of each poet of the past redeems the other as model. The artist can achieve impersonality, make a unique use of tradition which will give him an individuality or selfhood.' In an age with Alexandrian characteristics, it is necessary in Harold Bloom's phrase 'to become one with the redemptive imagination of the precursor'. This is a dialectic not of imitation of external characteristics but of impersonation, parody, caricature sometimes of the precursor. Peckham describes Swinburne's style in *Poems and Ballads* as one of 'non-expressive æsthetic', that is to say with a surface beauty that arrests penetration into the painful depths of content. This surface is won by Swinburne's control over many men's styles, and by numerous forms, including many modulations of rhymed stanzas, some distinctly unusual. It becomes fused by continuous usage of alliterations, assonances, patterns of repeated vowel noises, repeated syntactical patterns. That Swinburne intended this highly glazed reflexive surface, there can be no doubt. Often he strews epithets, simply for sound, as décor; tepid words such as 'sweet', found four times in a single stanza of 'A Ballad of Death', 'sad', 'pale', 'fair', 'bright', all contributing to the non-expressive surface. Sometimes as many as four epithets (which may be internally rhymed) exhaust their substantive. Such are not emotional shorthand merely, but

analogous rather to the many unaccented articles, con-
junctions and prepositions, which are designed to assure a
glancing rapidity of reading. The reader must, however, be
alert: 'As bones of men under the deep sharp sea', that
second epithet is witty, not decorative. Criticism has justly
observed that the diction of *Poems and Ballads* is rarely ornate.
Dismissed as overlush and decadent, Swinburne is, on the
contrary, according to John Rosenberg, the most *austere*
among the greatly gifted poets of the century:

> Oh yet would God this flesh of mine might be
> Where air might wash and long leaves cover me,
>   Where tides of grass break into foam of flowers,
> Or where the winds' feet shine along the sea.

A muster of monosyllables; he is indeed 'the supreme
master in English of the bleak beauty of little words'.

'The structure of the book', Swinburne himself commented, 'has been as carefully considered and arranged as I
could make it.' And in a pamphlet defending himself against
the reviewers, he wrote that:

the book is dramatic, many-faced, multifarious; and no utterance of
enjoyment or despair, belief or unbelief, can properly be assumed as
the assertion of its author's personal feeling or faith.

This is not necessarily history. But we may believe that
Swinburne made some attempt to distance the personal,
and he was obviously familiar with Baudelaire's ordering of
Les Fleurs du Mal into sections representing possible avenues
of escape from a modern *accidie*. The effect of *Poems and
Ballads* however, is rather that of a continuous monologue
which resounds through a number of masks.

Swinburne rationalized the 'fall' in terms of his mentors
Sade, Blake, and Baudelaire, and so furnished for the speaker
of *Poems and Ballads* an intellectual programme which has
been brilliantly analysed for us by Professor Julian Baird.
While Swinburne respected Sade as theologian, he was less
impressed by Sade as artist. Even as theologian, however,

Swinburne probably considered Sade inferior to Blake, for Sade persisted in that Christian dualism which distinguished between body and spirit. According to him the body is fulfilled only in filth, misery and cruelty by means of which the individual consciousness is engulfed in unity with another. In spite of Sade's anti-Christian polemics, his was mere despairing mortification of the flesh, not Pagan freedom. Blake, according to Swinburne's reading, realized that body and spirit were indivisible, 'body' should never be 'bruised to pleasure soul'; 'above all gods of creation and division, [Blake] beheld by faith in a perfect man a supreme God.' There was neither divine person nor divine thing but the human. But this insight needs to be won from a 'fallen' world of custom and restraint in which Christian immanence has retracted, but Nature's divinity is not admitted; rather, a transcendent and cruel creator is postulated. Against this 'new' Nature and this 'new Nature's god', man must rebel and himself become God:

God is man, and man God; as neither of himself the greater, so neither of himself the less: but as God is the unfallen part of man, man the fallen part of God, God must needs be (not more than man, but assuredly) more than the qualities of man. . . . The other 'God' . . . who created the sexual and separate body of man, did but cleave in twain the 'divine humanity', which becoming reunited shall redeem man without price and without covenant and without law; . . . meantime, the Creator is a divine demon, liable to error, subduable by and through this very created nature of his invention, which he for the present imprisons and torments.

(William Blake)

The ideal of *Poems and Ballads* is therefore a species of gnosticism. It institutes an attempt to transcend the dualism of spirit and matter and return to hermaphrodite unity, through a series of variations on the dominant theme of love, heterosexual, homosexual, oral-genital and sado-masochistic, a dialogue between the poems themselves.

The volume opens with two imitations of court ballads of 1500 odd, 'A Ballad of Life' corresponding to a Blakean state of innocence, which 'the poet-dreamer can appreciate as beautiful, but from which he is separated by intervening years and which he does not fully understand'. 'A Ballad of Death' represents Blake's state of Experience, 'a sorrowful waking state which takes full cognizance of the death of innocent physical love in a world which accepts laws for the flesh' (Baird). Both poems are addressed to Lucrezia Borgia: the first celebrates her as the divinity of matter, the second laments her death 'as a vesture with new dyes, / The body that was clothed with love of old'. The allusion is to that notion of Sacred and Profane Love, best known through Titian's famous painting, where sacred love has been interpreted as the naked, profane love as the clothed lady: shame comes with the 'fall'.[1] Lucrezia, in legend, had committed incest with father and brother, but here she is seen as representing purified nature, the love that must be distinguished behind the lineaments of lust. Emblem of unity, of Renaissance paganism, she becomes the first in a series of emblematic ladies, all of whom are judged in the light of the living Lucrezia. Figures such as Faustine and Dolores (no less than the 'nightmare life-in-death' of Coleridge, and Shelley's Medusa) mark the re-appearance in Romantic poetry of those dazzling witches of Romantic epic: Alcina, Acrasia and Armida. The Swinburne female represents the familiar paradoxical attempt to reconcile the Romantic antinomies: pleasure—pain; mystery—know-ledge; coition—death, and to preserve essence in a world of flickering phenomena. Essentially passive, she is both victim and victress: though the poet sacrifices himself to her, her gaze (like that of Yeats's ladies on unicorns, in 'Meditations in Time of Civil War'), is turned inwards, in an act of self-worship that becomes masochistic precisely because she has taken herself as object. Swinburne uses other literary commonplaces, but always in a strictly personalized

[1] See 'Sacred and Profane Love' in E. Wind, *Pagan Mysteries of the Renaissance*, 2nd and revised edition, 1967, for the complex history of interpretation.

manner: sexual, for example, as emblem of cosmic disorder. The varieties of love are symbolized by Venus as popular or heterosexual love, as homoerotic, as sapphic, and as Venus Anadyomene. In this last the sea is represented as sexual 'Mother and lover', older than history, beyond family and society, with whom one can intensify identity and yet be, as with other lovers one cannot, totally mingled, and whose embraces are at once more fatal and sexually keen than those of others.

'A Ballad of Death' concludes with a journey and a return:

> ... it may be
> That when thy feet return at evening
> Death shall come in with thee.

Even the proposed revise of the volume would not have assured that subtle placing, and cogent unfolding of poem after poem in dialogue with one another that we find in the maturity of Yeats. Yet a broad narrative line can be traced in *Poems and Ballads*. The end of 'A Ballad of Death' leads naturally on to 'Laus Veneris'. This poem relates the poet Tannhäuser's fruitless journey to Rome for absolution by the Pope from the sin of his service to Venus under the Venusberg.[1] The Pope refuses absolution and Tannhäuser returns to Venus. Originally a medieval legend, this tale had been retold several times in the nineteenth century, by Heine, Treck, in Wagner's opera (1849), and in Baudelaire's defence of the work twelve years later, while the subject became popular in England particularly in the *fin de siècle*.[2]

---

[1] The mountain which became the refuge of Venus after the defeat of the pagan gods by Christianity. Burne-Jones's lost watercolour of 1861 on the topic probably influenced Swinburne. A larger version of the theme in oil of 1873-8 has a Venus who was aptly described by a contemporary as 'wan and death-like, eaten up and gnawn away by disappointment and desire'. Its iridescent colours, 'shot' reds and golds, also connect with Swinburne's imagery.

[2] See, for example, John Davidson's 'A New Ballad of Tannhäuser' in *New Ballads* (1897); Herbert E. Clarke's *Tannhäuser and other Poems* (1896); Pater's allusions in the unpublished portions of *Gaston de Latour* and Beardsley's *Venus and Tannhäuser*.

The medieval setting recalls Heine's theory that the pagan gods after the triumph of Christianity either enlisted in the new religion or became demons.

In Swinburne's poem, written in a stricter variation of the metre used by Fitzgerald in his *Rubaiyat* (1859), we meet further literary commonplaces creatively distorted. The Venusberg, in its heat and aridity, resembles one of those false secondary Gardens of Eden that are found in Renaissance epic. 'The scented dusty daylight burns the air.' Just as temptation *creates* Spenser's Bower of Bliss (though the reader remains informed by imagery no less than by comment that it *is* illusion, infernal not paradisal), so Tannhäuser recreates Venus as succuba, notwithstanding his choice of her in place of Christ. In Julian Baird's reading, the situation is that of 'A Ballad of Life' inverted. In that poem the lover could distinguish the gold of love under the dusty overlayer of lust. For Tannhäuser, who believes in duality of body and spirit, love and lust remain the same, but individuated still. Thus as knight he believes in Christ, but as lover in Venus: here there is no epiphany of feminine purity, as in some versions of the Tannhäuser story. In the traditional false earthly Paradise the lover sleeps, while the insatiate succuba wakes. Here Venus sleeps with the lineaments of satisfied desire; the only sign of life is: 'a purple speck / Wherein the pained blood falters and goes out.' But Tannhäuser desires final death and judgement, associating Venus with the Great Harlot of Revelations.

> For till the thunder in the trumpet be,
> Soul may divide from body, but not we
>   One from another; . . .
>
> I seal myself upon thee with my might,
> Abiding always out of all men's sight
>   Until God loosen over the sea and land
> The thunder of the trumpets of the night.

This is the longing for confirmation of damnation experienced by the inverted Christian who cannot transcend what he hates and loves. The poem conforms also to the traditional romantic theme of the quest, and Tannhäuser's return journey mirrors the æsthetic pilgrim's penitential reversal.

Next in order there follows a fragment of dialogue between Phaedra and Hippolytus with choric interventions. If Tannhäuser remains strangely passive in love, Phaedra is aggressive, a woman obsessed with desire for her stepson, the victim of an unknown God who, like Death, cannot be appeased with gifts, or rather can only be appeased by the death of both Phaedra and Hippolytus. Phaedra's madness communicates itself through images of bestiality. The mother-son relationship precisely inverts that in *Atalanta in Calydon:* Hippolytus sacrifices himself to the false 'god' of custom and restraint. This is followed by three poems associated by Swinburne and bearing directly on the auto-biographical situation.

In 'The Triumph of Time', half allegory, half narrative, Swinburne speaks in his own voice. The poem is at once rapid in movement and long in proportion to its intellectual content, that length suggesting the processional rite of the 'Triumph' form as practised by poets from Petrarch to Shelley. The theme is the conspiracy of Fates, Gods and Time, again a love which is imaged sacramentally: 'This wild new growth of the corn and vine'; but the speaker learns that communion will be impossible; he is alone. Time, in traditional mode, acts as both destroyer of his love and revealer of his true situation.

The hermaphrodite image of innocent primitive unity, two bodies and souls, is invoked:

> Twain halves of a perfect heart, made fast
> Soul to soul while the years fell past;
>
> . . .
>
> But now, you are twain, you are cloven apart;
> Flesh of his flesh, but heart of my heart;
> And deep in one is the bitter root,
>   And sweet for one is the lifelong flower.

And so, to the marine Venus:

> O fair green-girdled mother of mine,
>> Sea, that art clothed with the sun and the rain,
> Thy sweet hard kisses are strong like wine,
>> Thy large embraces are keen like pain.
> Save me and hide me with all thy waves,
> Find me one grave of thy thousand graves,
> Those pure cold populous graves of thine,
>> Wrought without hand in a world without stain.

Late in the poem, to generalize the adolescent fantasy of dying for the loved one, Swinburne recalls the Troubadour Rudel who fell in love with the Princess of Tripoli, set out for her duchy, saw her and died in her smile.

> There lived a singer in France of old
>> By the tideless, dolorous midland sea.
> In a land of sand and ruin and gold
>> There shone one woman, and none but she.

(The Troubadours were viewed in the nineteenth century as the originators of romantic love.)

The second poem, 'Les Noyades', presents a similar strategy; this is a rapid balladish version of an incident from the French Revolution which had been vividly reported by Carlyle. Carrier, an agent of the Revolution, is sent to suppress a revolt in Nantes. To dispose of the numerous prisoners he adopts a 'final solution', having many supporters of the *ancien régime* placed on board ships on the Loire which are then sunk: 'daylight . . . witnesses Noyades: women and men are tied together, feet and feet, hands and hands; and flung in: this they call *Mariage Républicain*.' In Swinburne, though nowhere else, Carrier appears as a destructive androgyne: 'A queen of men, with helmeted hair.' A young worker and a noble 'maiden, wonderful, white' are bound together and the young man exults in this consummation through death. The speaker in the poem breaks away from the past into the present and imagines himself and his lost love being driven down from the Loire to the sea:

> We should yield, go down, locked hands and feet,
> Die, drown together, and breath catch breath;

but the poem twists at the end:

> But you would have felt my soul in a kiss,
> . . .
> And I would have given my soul for this
> To burn for ever in burning hell.

The last poem of this trilogy, 'The Leave Taking', is cere-
moniously controlled, but concludes with the same wish,
dissolution in the sea. The theme of incest and sacrifice is
pursued in 'Itylus'. 'Anactoria', which follows, is a monologue of the Lesbian poet Sappho modelled on the tirades
of Ovid's 'Sappho to Phaon' and Pope's baroque 'Eloisa to
Abelard'. The couplets often fall into an Augustan mode,
in which the balanced phrases are underscored by
alliteration:

> Bade sink the spirit and the flesh aspire,
> Pain animate the dust of dead desire,

Sappho's obsession with Anactoria's image is mimed in the
recurring rhymes of some couplets which fracture Augustan
decorum. Sappho represents the most frenetic example of
the desire to restore primitive unity by means of a violent
mingling with the beloved, but love turns to the wish to
violate what is loved, as in the witty couplet which trans-
forms sterile love into art:

> Take thy limbs living, and new-mould with these
> A lyre of many faultless agonies?

But art too is as sterile as its emblem, love for Anactoria.
Sappho's hatred extends to 'the mute melancholy lust of
heaven' and God: 'Him would I reach, him smite, him
desecrate.' Finally, self-violation ensues, and Sappho hurls
herself into the 'insuperable' sea. 'Anactoria' had touched
on the failure of immortality through art; death and immortality are the themes of the 'Hymn to Proserpine', a

monologue spoken by a Pagan at the close of the ancient world, who is caught between worlds.

In 'Hermaphroditus' Swinburne exploits a Pre-Raphaelite derangement of a tradition, that of lyrics and sonnets which are closely related to the visual arts.[1] Like Rossetti, Swinburne does not use the genre merely to exalt art over nature, or to argue a hierarchy of arts or make a 'picturesque' attempt to reproduce visual effects in language. Rossetti, for example, invariably *interprets* the image, relating his poem to a particular work of art, considered as capturing 'a moment's monument'. 'Hermaphroditus' is based on a statue in the Louvre with female breasts and male genitals, reclining on a couch in ambiguous posture. The literary source is Ovid's recounting of the tale of Salmacis and Hermaphroditus who blend into one androgynous being in water. Rossetti had described picture and poem as bearing 'the same relation to each other as beauty does in man and woman: the point of meeting where the two are identical is the supreme perfection.' The 'beauty' of the picture is reciprocated by the 'identical'—if superficially dissimilar—'beauty' of the poem resulting in an indivisible ideal unity, comparable only to the state of love. In Rossetti's sonnets for pictures of women, the metaphor is actualized as an encounter between observer-poet and portrait-beloved. Swinburne's own prose interpretation connects 'Hermaphroditus' with art and the artist. Of his friend Simeon Solomon's painting 'My Soul and I' Swinburne wrote: '[It] contains both the idea of the separation of male and female qualities and their union as body and soul . . .'. And of Solomon's iconography in general, 'In almost all of these there is perceptible the same profound suggestion of . . . the identity of contraries'. (Swinburne's 'Erotion' originated in a picture of Solomon's.) The Pre-Raphaelite hermaphrodite stems from

[1] The genre goes back to Homer's Shield of Achilles, the sixteenth book of the Greek Anthology and to Renaissance 'gallery' poems. Typically, Swinburne parodies Rossetti's sonnets for pictures.

the male-female union of the epiphany of the woman soul
to the young painter in Rossetti's 'Hand and Soul'.[1]
Swinburne's response is poised between the optimism and
pessimism that the hermaphrodite image generated in the
nineteenth century:

> A strong desire begot on great despair,
> A great despair cast out by strong desire.

'Fragoletta' or 'little strawberry' prolongs the same theme
and is followed by two poems that introduce the tyrannies
of the religion of law: 'A Litany' presents an Old Testament
God who speaks a threatening first antiphon and the human
response slavishly echoes both syntax and rhyme. 'Faustine',
a *tour de force* of forty-one stanzas, pivoting on the proper
name at the end of each, is another critical presentation of
the Fatal Woman: the transformation of a contemporary
into the Empress Faustine, beautiful and vicious in legend.
Like all Fatal Women, continuously reincarnated, she
becomes victim of men's images of her. In his notes,
Swinburne refers to her as 'doomed as though by accident
from the first to all evil and no good, through many ages
and forms, but clad always in the same type of fleshly
beauty'. This is followed by another poem for a painting
'Before the Mirror' designed to accompany Whistler's 'The
Little White Girl', which shows a girl in profile leaning on
a mantelpiece while her reflection in three-quarter view in
the mirror reveals a pensive, perhaps suffering expression.
The elegy for Landor and the Ode to one of Swinburne's
constant heroes, Victor Hugo, celebrate two figures who
championed private and public liberty and so extend the
concept of freedom from the religious to the social and
political plane. At this climactic stage of *Poems and Ballads*
we encounter three closely inter-related poems: 'Dolores',
'The Garden of Proserpine' and 'Hesperia'.

'Dolores' is the most notorious poem of the volume, a
lyric of frenzied negations devoted to the Madonna of

---

[1] Another source is Gautier's *Mademoiselle de Maupin*.

Sado-masochism, a parody almost of the Fatal Woman theme: Medusa's or Lamia's head has become suspiciously similar to that of King Charles. In 'Faustine', 'Les Noyades' or 'Laus Veneris' we witness the transformation by guilt of woman from either past or present into *femme fatale*. In 'Dolores' the image in itself is convoked. Each individual stanza is possessed by that rhythm of tumescence and detumescence that flows and ebbs through 'Anactoria'. His letters indicate that Swinburne sometimes considered 'Dolores' as a 'black' joke: 'Thy skin changes country and colour, / And shrivels or swells to a snake's.' The poem ends with the promise that death will bring 'the joys of thee seventy times seven, / Our Lady of Pain,' regardless of any belief or blankness about immortality, Hell or Heaven. The conclusion of 'Anactoria' is parodied. The coda is exhaustion, but also purgation. In 'The Garden of Proserpine', Thanatos, a severe Greek angel, is welcome after Eros in all his wilder shapes:

> Pale, beyond porch and portal,
>   Crowned with calm leaves, she stands
> Who gathers all things mortal
>   With cold immortal hands; . . .
>
> She waits for each and other,
>   She waits for all men born . . .
>
> From too much love of living,
>   From hope and fear set free,
> We thank with brief thanksgiving
>   Whatever Gods may be
> That no life lives for ever;
> That dead men rise up never;
> That even the weariest river
>   Winds somewhere safe to sea.

'Hesperia' alludes to that land in the west of the fortunate dead and pleasant memories, reigned over by Proserpine. The poem's rhythms contrast with its two predecessors by slow authority, as of sea music, the second short half of

every first and third line finishing with an inflexing feminine
rhyme, the breaking wave. After the feral interiors of
'Dolores' and the windless void of Proserpine's Garden, the
reascent from the experiences recorded in the whole volume
is marked now by memories of wind and the sea, of wild
riding and, associated with the healing presence of the Venus
Anadyomene, of the one woman who underlay all images
of loss, hatred and compensation:

> Thee I behold as a bird borne in with the wind from the west,
> Straight from the sunset, across white waves whence rose as a
> > daughter
> Venus thy mother, in years when the world was a water at rest.

transfigured now synaesthesically into a Muse: 'Thy silence
as music, thy voice as an odour that fades in a flame.' The
speaker hopes that the loved woman will understand and
pity, but not love, for love, he has proved, is 'As the cross
that a wild nun clasps till the edge of it bruises her bosom'
(validating the comparison of 'Anactoria' with 'Eloisa and
Abelard'). Dolores is transcended and the poem concludes
with a memory of Swinburne's reckless horse-riding with
Mary, creating a future of its own.

The two translated love songs that follow are of appropriate lightness; 'Félise', a dramatic monologue, is spoken
by a young man to a somewhat older woman, after a year's
absence from one another. Swinburne commented that he
had expressed their story 'Plainly and "cynically" enough!
Last year I loved you Félise and you were puzzled, and
didn't love me—quite.' The poem affects the reader—as
other diffused poems do not—as over-elongated, though
the young man is playing rather cruelly. The intention is to
present a new 'mask', one of control over the personality,
but the drift into a familiar anti-theism undercuts the
objectivity. 'Hendecasyllabics'—following an 'Interlude' of
spring—has art, winter and endurance as its themes and,
like its companion piece, 'Sapphics', the stress on exercise
indicates distance and control. 'Sapphics' also 'corrects'

'Anactoria' in its ritual, chastened version of Sappho's
death:

> By the grey sea-side, unassuaged, unheard of,
> Unbeloved, unseen in the ebb of twilight,
> Ghosts of outcast women return lamenting,
> Purged not in Lethe.

The loose progression of the volume is continued with the
ballads whose subject foreshadows that of Swinburne's next
major work, *Atalanta in Calydon*, in paiticular that of 'The
Bloody Son', a tale of fratricide and exile. The new work
will centre on the tyranny (and death) of the family.

V

To write a play in the style of the Greek tragic poets was
not unusual in nineteenth-century England; but the form
was often used to evade the realities of the contemporary
scene. Swinburne, however, used it to confront, if
obliquely, his own age. The principal sources for *Atalanta
in Calydon* are Homer, Ovid's *Metamorphoses* and the extant
fragments of Euripides' *Meleager*. The legend runs: Althaea,
Queen of Calydon, pregnant with her first child, Meleager,
dreams that she has given birth to a firebrand. The Three
Fates attend his birth and prophesy that he will be strong
and fortunate and will live as long as a brand which is at that
time in the fire. His mother plucks out the brand and guards
it. While Meleager is away with Jason's Argonauts, his
father King Oeneus sacrifices to all the gods but Artemis.
In revenge, Artemis stirs up various tribes to fight against
the Calydonians, and becomes still more angry when
Oeneus defeats his enemies. She then sends a wild boar to
Calydon which ravages the land, killing many who attempt
to hunt it down. Men come from all over Greece to try
their hand at destroying this beast. With them comes

Atalanta, a virgin, and one who is highly favoured by
Artemis. For Atalanta's sake, Artemis allows the boar to be
killed. Atalanta pierces the beast with her spear and then
Meleager kills it, presenting its carcass to Atalanta, with
whom he has fallen in love. Althaea's brothers, Toxeus and
Plexippus, who have already grumbled hugely about
Atalanta's presence on the hunt, attempt to take the spoil
from her, but Meleager protects Atalanta and kills the pair
of them. On hearing this, Althaea in a frenzy of rage takes
the brand and throws it into the fire. As the brand is consumed, so Meleager wastes away and dies and his mother
dies soon after him, broken with grief, though in Swinburne's play she suffers a 'symbolic' death only.

Swinburne's *Atalanta* can be structurally related to the
formal design of Greek tragedy: Prologos, Parodos, Episode,
Stasimon, Exodos. Of the three extant tragic poets, he
apparently most admired Aeschylus; but to detect Aeschylus
as model is difficult. Swinburne does not use the chorus as a
narrator nor does he attempt any Aeschylean reconciliation
of human and divine order. At the close of the *Oresteia*,
moreover, the old goddesses, the Furies, are subdued by new
patriarchal gods; in *Atalanta*, the female principle triumphs,
nominally Artemis, though there must be doubt as to her
precise nature, while the symbolic destruction of Althaea
qualifies the triumph. Some have proffered unconvincing
Sophoclean readings of the play as asserting a 'golden mean'
which Althaea, Atalanta and Meleager all violate: but this
would deny the work any modern element. Swinburne is
closer to Euripides in sometimes using the chorus as lyrical
refreshment or mirror of the action. The chorus beginning
'O that I now, I too were / By deep wells and water-floods'
clearly recalls the famous chorus in the *Hippolytus:* 'Would
that I might hide in the secret heart of a cloud,' representing
a similar moment of evasion. There is, however, no *deus ex
machina* in *Atalanta*. More broadly, Swinburne's moral tone
is often as mysterious as that of Euripides.[1]

[1] Oddly enough, as Swinburne detested that 'Zola of the fifth century'.

In *Atalanta* the chorus sometimes gives a lyrical formulation to the inner feelings of the protagonists. They begin with the innocently hopeful 'When the hounds of spring are on winter's traces', chanted at dawn: if light follows dark, spring, winter—the boar must surely be killed. This motif is counterpointed immediately by Althaea's assertion of a determined cycle of pain and pleasure to which men's lives are confined. Even in the opening chorus, however, the implication of such a cycle troubles the imagery: 'scare / The wolf that follows, the fawn that flies', resolved by Althaea's 'Night, a black hound, follows the white fawn day.' Criticism has remarked a further structural element: the conflict between the dialectic public world of the iambic metre and the dionysiac world of the choric. The chorus's exuberance dwindles finally to a curt bleak utterance: the lords of life, whoever they may be, have a kingdom of 'strong hands', reflecting on the pitiful manly strength of Meleager and the brothers (and perhaps on the pitiful diminutiveness of Swinburne himself).

This larger structural device is supported by iterative imagery. Swinburne has as usual been accused here of infatuation with certain words, but the repetitions are deliberate and regulated: Night/day; spring/winter; male/female; flower/blossom/bud; hard/soft; and are invoked in the persons of Artemis and Apollo at the play's onset, moon and sun. Contrapuntal words which dominate are 'fire' associated with Althaea, and 'snow' and 'whiteness' which are Atalanta's property as surrogate of Artemis. But these images are not polarized merely, they are also ambiguous in the play's plural world. Fire is alluded to as purging disease—the boar is to be 'consumed'; but fire also destroys life, Meleager's life. Atalanta is a snowy *rose*. In terms of character, Althaea is passionate and unforgiving; Atalanta for all her desolating purity is still capable of pity.

> Hail thou: but I with heavy face and feet
> Turn homeward and am gone out of thine eyes.

The simplest reading of the play is to isolate Althaea as agent in a *Sons and Lovers* situation. Swinburne was fascinated by matriarchal, aristocratic figures subtly controlling their families. Althaea is a tragic version of the ruthless anti-romantic Lady Midhurst of *Love's Cross Currents*. Among Swinburne's aims in *Atalanta*, however, was that of excluding the overtly modern and discursive. To achieve this he had to subdue the autobiographical and the amusement of attacking the Christian God under veil of complaint about the Greek pantheon. To be sure, Althaea and Meleager are pivotal figures: Althaea is both passionately and intensely stoical, distrustful of the gods. For her, life has 'much to be endured and little to be enjoyed'. One must be wary, attempt to sustain patterns of civility, kingdom and family, our only refuge in a cruel world: the Victorian parallels are clear. She belongs with those who practice restraint and distrust nature. Her husband King Oeneus plays an oddly muted part. A compromiser, past his best, he attempts to mediate with 'soft obstetric hand' between Meleager and Althaea:

> Nor thee I praise, who art fain to undo things done:
> Nor thee, who art swift to esteem them overmuch.

These well-meaning banalities are futile. Althaea's two brothers are presented rather as rugger club hearties, thrusting their virility at everyone. On Atalanta, their genial comment is that the only justification for virgins is that their throats can be cut for purposes of sacrifice. Such beefy conservatism strongly contrasts with the intelligent conservatism of Althaea. Swinburne was not one of those arrogant radicals who assume that all reactionaries are by definition stupid.

Atalanta herself has all the passivity of the Fatal Woman: she does not tempt Meleager, though it is through her that Althaea and Artemis destroy him. Indeed, Althaea co-operates with Meleager in creating Atalanta's Fatal Woman aspect:

She the strange woman, she the flower, the sword,
Red from spilt blood, a mortal flower to men,
Adorable, detestable—even she
Saw with strange eyes and with strange lips rejoiced.

Does Althaea detect some numinous tinge about Atalanta?
She fears her because Atalanta is literally a stranger, a
foreigner, outside the warm structure of family and kingdom but, more profoundly, strange as a virgin by vocation,
one who lives in the white shadow of Artemis. Atalanta has
evaded the roles that give woman social identity: she does
not weave and breed as do other women: she hunts with
men. But Althaea is also distrustful of romantic love as
such; it is, by Greek tradition, a disaster; its strict cor-
relative, pain, so the chorus chant: 'For an evil blossom is
born / Of sea-foam and the frothing of blood', alluding
apparently to Aphrodite's birth (and Atalanta's effect on
Meleager) but with dramatic irony defining Althaea: 'For
they knew thee for mother of love, / And knew thee not
mother of death.'

What of Meleager's attitudes? A plausible suggestion is
that he represents the æstheticism so eloquently expressed in
Pater's 'Conclusion' to Studies in the History of the Renaissance.
Meleager too recognizes the inevitability of a pleasure-pain
cycle, that life becomes more flame-like from the fact that
'each man, dying, is earth and shadow; the nothing sinks
into nothingness' to cite that fragment from Euripides'
Meleager which Swinburne prefixed to his play. Meleager's
response is that the individual must seize on the good
moment before the cycle returns to pain. He embodies the
Dionysiac reverberation of the opening chorus: not to lay
hold of joy 'on this short day of frost and sun,' is 'to sleep
before evening.' But that seizure precisely brings Meleager
to sleep before evening; it is the dim Oeneus who survives.
Yet Meleager chooses joy, love, and, it has been suggested,
in Paterian mode, art. At the close of the Greek play which
Atalanta most resembles, the Hippolytus of Euripides, as the
virgin Artemis leaves the dying hero, he addresses her as a

Madonna come to witness his *pietà*: 'thou leavest me now, blessed virgin', but Artemis is void of power to ease his pain; she can say only that if gods could weep, she would. Hippolytus asks the human auditors to cover his face with his cloak that he may retain dignity in the last anguish. Atalanta, a mortal, though Artemis' double, can feel pity and more. Meleager asks her:

> But thou, dear, hide my body with thy veil,
> And with thy raiment cover foot and head,
> And stretch thyself upon me and touch hands
> With hands and lips with lips. . . .

It is a traditional orgasm-as-death passage (very close to a similar passage in Tasso's *Aminta;* but also to Wagner's *Tristan*): Meleager does not die alone; this is communion, a life-enhancing ritual moment; life measured not by length but intensity; life as the end of life, in this mime of the sexual act, a ghostly Eros. Pater is again relevant: 'With this sense of the splendour of our experience and of its awful brevity, gathering all we are into one desperate effort to see and touch.' Such insight brings Meleager joy and death. He forgives Althaea, recognizing that she can only act out the antinomies of her role:

> thou too, queen,
> The source and end, the sower and the scythe,
> The rain that ripens and the drought that slays . . .
> To make me and unmake thou—thou, I say,
> Althaea, since my father's ploughshare, drawn
> Through fatal seedbed of a female field
> Furrowed thy body. . . I
> Hail thee as holy and worship thee as just
> Who art unjust and unholy . . .
> . . . me too thou hast loved, and I
> Thee; but this death was mixed with all my life,
> Mine end with my beginning.

Althaea in destroying Meleager destroys her role and herself: 'I am severed from myself, my name is gone,' and employing for the last time the image of fire: 'My name that was a healing, it is changed / My name is a consuming. / From this time . . . / My lips shall not unfasten till I die.' So she has no words for Meleager's last speech. As Professor L. Wymer observes, she suffers a death-in-life which epiphanizes her past life and role. Ironically, she has become her own image of Atalanta: a stranger to herself and her son. The play, indeed, abounds with the words 'division', 'cleave': in Meleager's dying speech, for example, 'I sprang and cleft the closure of thy womb.'

The ancient form acts as challenge and discipline: Swinburne achieved in *Atalanta in Calydon* an effect paralleled by *Samson Agonistes*. In either case, the poet without violating the Greek norms arrives at a highly personal tragic insight. Just as Milton's blindness gave acuity to his drama of temptation, so Swinburne's peculiar psychology enables him to realize the price that a weak-bodied æsthete must pay in a world without gods or personal immortality.

VI

Many nineteenth-century poets were deeply involved in romantic politics. Reacting from the Enlightenment and its instrument, the internationalist French Revolution, there emerged a nationalism of the 'sacred soil', of ancestors 'who stemmed with their own bodies' the invader. Nations were defined by wars of independence, first in Germany, then on that most sacred soil of all, the Greek. Byron's effort and death for Hellenism became profoundly symbolic. The 'Young Ireland' group of poets and politicians, the Italian *Risorgimento* form part of this same vivid movement. The first phase of the *Risorgimento* or 'resurrection', associated with Swinburne's master, Mazzini, was, however, strongly tinged with notions from the Enlightenment. But by the later 1860s, when Swinburne was composing most of his *Songs before Sunrise*, the Italian struggle had mutated into a more narrow nationalism.

Songs before Sunrise is Swinburne's celebration of the *Risorgimento* as it moved towards its climax in the loss by 'Pius Iscariot' (so Swinburne called Pio Nono) of the Patrimony of Peter to the kingdom of Italy. The models are Whitman and Hugo's *Les Châtiments*. Swinburne's republican zeal can be detected as early as 1852, the date of his first surviving political poem. The strategy of *Songs before Sunrise* is to appropriate the rhetoric of ecclesiastical tyranny to dignify Italy and republicanism. Despite the political reality, the *Risorgimento* is presented there as part of a world process, in which man creates himself God through aggregation to a perfect society: 'Love, the beloved republic.' These notions were widespread among 'advanced' men of letters. As one of Swinburne's contemporaries put it:

Every great poet of the last half century is loud in this demand for liberty of passion and liberty of action—freedom of the individual will. But if the individual be thus free, what guarantee is there that he will not injure his neighbour and reduce society to chaos? The answer is that love is the harmonizer of the passions, and that large idea of friendship— the universal brotherhood of democracy — the harmonizer of human action.[1]

Italy becomes Madonna, the people Christ; the republic, a Christ in the tomb. This rhetoric (its polemics have interesting connexions with those of Blake) functions sometimes successfully, sometimes with results as grotesque as those of Crashaw's deliberate confusions of spiritual and physical: in 'Blessed Among Women' we learn that Italy is 'four times blest, / At whose most holy breast / Four times a godlike soldier-saviour hung.'

The contents fall into three broad categories, the weakest celebrating topical events in the war for liberty. 'The Ride to Milan' veers towards doggerel; the Odes are tumid merely. But the quasi-philosophic poems such as 'Genesis', 'Mater Triumphalis' and 'Hertha' which combine evolutionary themes with a mystical pantheism, are surprisingly

[1] John Todhunter, Reading University MS 202/4/3/1.

impressive. 'Hertha', for example, asserts the Mother-
creative principle against the false Creator-god of Blake,
who seeks to limit men, by imposing on him the identity of
a servant. Yet it is when all large abstractions melt into
some sense of the sacred actualities of Italy, as in 'Siena'
(evoking St Catherine of Siena's voluptuous trances of a
vicarious suffering, no less than her public role as rebuker
of great men and mentor of Popes); or in the inevitable but
still piercing comparison of Italy with Israel in bondage,
'Super Flumen Babylonis', that Swinburne remains most
moving. In 'Christmas Antiphonies', he appropriates the
Christian form of the carol with a conspicuous success. And
the rhythms are subtle still as in this stylized grief, some
peasant woman released by the wordless rocking of the
body:

> Who is this that sits by the way, by the wild wayside,
> In a rent stained garment, the robe of a cast-off bride,
> In the dust, in the rainfall sitting, with soiled feet bare,
> With the night for a garment upon her, with torn wet hair?
> She is fairer of face than the daughters of men, and her eyes,
> Worn through with her tears are deep as the depth of skies.

('Mater Dolorosa')

Swinburne perhaps had reservations about Mazzini's
practical failure: his distrust of materialism (and so of
material means). There is a curious episode in *Lesbia Brandon*
involving Mazzini's surrogate Attilio Mariani. Of Mariani
we read that 'even the sublime vanity of martyrs has its
weak side' and on his death he bequeathes the hero two
books, whose titles point to contradictions in Mazzini's
personality: the memoirs of Orsini and *La Chartreuse de Parme*.

VII

Few people think of Swinburne as the author of prose
fiction, yet he published one striking *nouvelle*, *Love's Cross
Currents*, while two substantial fragments *The Chronicle of
Tebaldeo Tebaldei* and *Lesbia Brandon* have since been edited

from manuscript. There is a short story, 'Dead Love', in Morris's early manner; a considerable fragment of a novel in French and two shorter highly amusing French burlesques: *La Fille du Policeman*, a tale, and an unfinished play *La Sœur de la Reine*.

Written early in the 1860s, *Love's Cross Currents* appeared in serial (and abbreviated) form in 1877 under the pseudonym of Mrs Horace Manners, possibly on account of its situations representing a refinement of those played out in the Isle of Wight between Swinburnes and Gordons. *Love's Cross Currents* offers us an aristocratic family group, complexly interrelated with violent emotions of hate and affinity, but with its members necessarily united against the bourgeois world. After a prologue detailing the web of relationships, the narrative is unfolded through letters in the manner made popular in the eighteenth century. The two principal figures are Lady Midhurst, now in her early sixties, ruthless, intelligent, patrician heir of the Enlightenment, and Mrs Clara Radworth in her later twenties, less intelligent, more passionate, married to a dull husband and impatient of the family game. These two ladies conduct a struggle over one of Lady Midhurst's grandchildren, Reginald Harewood (a character who bears some resemblance to the author). Reginald, responding to some not too veiled encouragement, has fallen in love with Clara. Lady Midhurst wishes to break this relationship partly because it threatens family stability, partly because she is fond of Reginald. That the affair is so far technically innocent is irrelevant: it may provoke a scandal. Moreover, the role of lap-dog barely suits Redgie's style: it makes him much less amusing. Lady Midhurst's other problem is her granddaughter, Reginald's half-sister, who has married Clara's cousin, Lord Cheyne (with whom Clara has herself been in love). Amicia, a dim glimmering creature of Pre-Raphaelite aspect, possibly echoes Rossetti's wife Lizzie Siddall. She and Clara's brother Frank had once loved one another, meet again, have an affair. The plot becomes as

tortuous as any Restoration comedy of intrigue and is
drastically resolved. Lord Cheyne is drowned and Frank
inherits the great house and title. Clara believes she has
triumphed doubly over Lady Midhurst. But Lady Midhurst
then discloses that Amicia is pregnant, actually by Frank
who, though all the family become aware of the child's
true father, loses by his own precipitancy both house and
title. A suavely bullying Lady Midhurst now dissolves her
other problem by threatening to show Redgie some letters
written by Clara when infatuated with a Frenchman.
These will conflict with the image Clara has imposed on
her admirer. Clara is forced to send Redgie about his
business in cold terms.

Though the tone of *Love's Cross Currents* is French rather
than English, its social ambiance is immediately convincing:
Swinburne really knew those country houses. Finely
characterized though Mrs Radworth is, Lady Midhurst
with her tart brilliance is among the most pungent characters in the Victorian novel, sustaining comparison with the
Countess de Saldar, Mrs Brookenham or even Becky Sharp.
Swinburne evokes her in rich phrase: 'she worried him with
dexterous feline mouth' (Lady Midhurst at the dinner table).
A character in *Lesbia Brandon* mistakenly opines that 'she is
nothing now but husks and fangs'. Clara is equally over-
confident and mistaken when she observes that Lady
Midhurst has 'fallen into a sort of hashed style, between a
French *portière* and a Dickens nurse', for Lady Midhurst is
always stylish, even when, after Cheyne's death, she gives
her tepid grand-daughter stoical advice. We may believe
that Swinburne endorses every Pagan word: 'All slavish-
ness, whether of body or spirit, leaves a taint where it
touches. It is as bad to be servile to God as it is to be servile
to man. Accept what you must accept, and obey where you
must obey, but make no pretence of a free-will offering.'
More characteristic is the radiant malice in her dismissal of
Clara over whom she not merely triumphs by letter, but
actually visits to enjoy the æsthetics of a visible defeat.

To use her own style, she is *dead beat*, and quite safe; viciously re-
signed. . . . She would have racked me if she could, no doubt, but
received me smiling from the tips of her teeth outward, and with a soft
dry pressure of the fingers. Not a hint of anything kept back. . . . I have
no doubt she will set all her wits to work and punish him for her failure.
She will hardly get up a serious affair again, or it might be a charity to
throw her some small animal by way of lighter food. It would not
surprise me if she fell to philanthropic labour, or took some devotional
drug by way of stimulant. The *bureau d'amourettes* is a bankrupt concern,
you see: her sensation-shop is closed for good. I prophesy she will turn
a decent, worrying wife of the simpler Anglican breed; home-keeping,
sharp-edged, earnestly petty and drily energetic. Negro-worship now,
or foreign missions, will be about her mark: perhaps too a dash and
sprinkle of religious feeling, with the chill just off; with a mild pinch of
the old Platonic mixture now and then to flavour and leaven her dead
lump of life. . . . Pity she had not more stock in hand to start with.

The success of *Love's Cross Currents* owes much to the dry
clarity enforced on it by the epistolary form: the 'avenging
buds of the birch' barely emerge and Swinburne's perpetual
awareness of the in-breeding subject is muted and
comically modulated. He preserves all the immediacy of
the novel in letters while the range of characters is sufficient
to evade the implausibilities inherent in the form which
troubled the eighteenth-century practitioners. Among mid-
Victorian fiction it remains unique: a welcome alternative
to the prevailing idealism or didacticism; a relief from the
heavy 'æsthetic teaching' of a George Eliot.

Lesbia Brandon is a more ambitious work, but too frag-
mentary to grasp as a whole. Swinburne is inconsistent
about dates and dates are important there, while the family
interrelationships have become still more dramatically
intricate: Denham, the tutor, in himself an interesting
creation, in love with Lady Warriston, after some years
somewhat implausibly becomes her lover, and the aged
sadistic Linley (a male counterpart of Lady Midhurst without her affections) reveals that Denham is Lady Warriston's
half-brother, a disclosure quite in the mode of contemporary
'sensation' novelists such as Mrs Braddon. There is a distinct

sense of *déja vu*: this cerebral androgyne, this sadistic tutor, the sexual play of sister with pretty younger brother—all have been met before, expressed with more authority, in *Poems and Ballads*. But *Lesbia Brandon* reads well. Lady Midhurst makes a subordinate but vivid appearance; the lengthy fragment is full of a sharp and detailed eloquence of landscape and psychological casuistry: Linley with his 'horrible delicacy of ear'; Denham, frustrated in his love, beating Lady Warriston's young brother with additional savagery because of the haunting difference between Herbert and his sister. Herbert's dream is a brilliant adolescent case study:

He saw the star of Venus, white and flower-like as he had always seen it, turn into a white rose and come down out of heaven, with a reddening centre that grew as it descended liker and liker a living mouth; but instead of desire he felt horror and sickness at the sight of it, and averted his lips with an effort to utter some prayer or exorcism; vainly for the dreadful mouth only laughed, and came closer. And cheek or chin, eyebrow or eye there was none; only this mouth.

Was Swinburne an important novelist *manqué*? Possibly the more objective form of the novel might have distanced the aggressively autobiographical had he persisted. Could he have achieved a *bildungsroman*? I incline to doubt, though we must regret that the impossibility of an audience constrained him finally to abandon *Lesbia Brandon*, which is best regarded as the brilliant detritus of the poetry of the middle sixties. When that poetry was written, there was little need for the novel, yet one would surely be content to exchange most of Swinburne's later verse for an achieved *Lesbia Brandon*.

VIII

That later verse can be summarily discussed. The second series of *Poems and Ballads* is a good miscellaneous volume: some pieces such as 'Ave Atque Vale', a dreamily eloquent memorial poem on Baudelaire whose theme reverses that of 'Laus Veneris', were written in the middle 1860s. Another admirable poem 'The Forsaken Garden' has been well described as 'symbolizing a total world beyond death and time realized through art alone': first of a kind of ideal autobiographical musing over those earlier years when his emotional life had been most intense: 'What lies before me is my past.' In such a vein, Swinburne nearly always writes commandingly: 'Thalassius' and 'On the Cliffs' in later collections. This volume contains also a distinguished group of translations from Villon though Swinburne discreetly replaced certain lines by asterisks in his published version of 'La Belle Heaulmière'.

Four years later appeared the last major volume, *Tristram of Lyonesse and Other Poems*. In the title poem Swinburne 'overgoes' Tennyson's 'Idylls of the Prince Consort', particularly 'The Last Tournament' of 1871 where Tristram and Iseult as servants of Tennyson's cautionary tale against adultery become coarse echoes of Launcelot and Guenevere: emblems of the autumnal moment of Arthur's Court. By contrast, Swinburne presents them as guiltless, absolute for love, and wins a nice debating point by recounting how Modred is the fruit of Arthur's adultery with Morgause. Tennyson's presentation of Mark is nastily effective; Swinburne presents the King sympathetically, so intensifying the love-hate role of Iseult of Brittany. The architectonic of *Tristram of Lyonesse* depends on a cyclic rhythm of months and the larger rhythms of the sea acting out a tragic determinism. The repetition of certain words and phrases has been not inaptly compared with the *leitmotifs* of Wagner's luscious opera: sea, rose, flame, molten, melting and the image of unity through the four lips of the lovers becoming at the close of the first canto 'one burning mouth' and 'one silent mouth' at the last. Orgasm and death are associated, but with more tragic authority than in *Poems and Ballads*. The poem is too long: the third canto and the interspersed lyrics are mediocre, the diction not always satisfying. Still, despite all 'languors and ardours', a strong and rapid narrative line remains; the metre acts like a funnel; the pace of the language carries one along and, for once, physical love is fulfilment. This prolonged hymn to erotic consummation remains the last irradiation of Swinburne's youth. From then on, though often skilful, Swinburne has increasingly less to say. Occasionally, he hits on a new theme. It has been noted that he adds to the image of Pan so popular in the second half of the nineteenth century. In the three later poems devoted to the god, 'A Nympholept', 'Pan and Thalassus' and 'The Palace of Pan', the goat-foot becomes ambiguous, close to Pater's presentation of Dionysus and Apollo. In Swinburne's version of him, Pan brings both terror and ecstasy, good and evil,—so evading any sentimentalizing of nature.

IX

Most of the great English critics have been practising poets; immediate examples comprise Ben Jonson, Dryden, Dr Johnson, Wordsworth, Coleridge, Keats, Arnold and Yeats. To this select group, Swinburne belongs, though important rather than great in his criticism. T. S. Eliot has aptly summarized its virtues: Swinburne had read widely and discriminatingly. And with the great critics, he has this in common: one senses that the whole European literary tradition is for him a continuous presence. His value judgements are firm and lasting. Eliot has pointed also to Swinburne's defects: his language, sometimes suggesting falsetto parody of his verse; hectic alliteration tangling with florid insult and rapture; his impatience with carrying through analysis; his refusal to focus rigorously on individual lines or images to make general points.

Such limitations partly rise from Swinburne's canons of criticism, which are both neo-classic and romantic. Neo-classic in that he believed in critical justice; in treating a

work as a whole and in conversing with the reader by
stating the pervasive general truth. This saves him from the
disjunctive approach to Elizabethan drama of Lamb and
other earlier romantic critics, with their distillation of
'specimens' and 'beauties'. Like Lamb, however, Swinburne
is rarely aware that his texts are documents of the theatre,
created mostly under conditions of actual staging, not in
some Parnassian air-pump. In his later criticism particularly,
Swinburne assumed the mannerism of Augustan prose with
its pomp of periphrasis. His romantic aspect appears in an
open-mindedness to originality, innovation and difficulty.
He was an enthusiast for Chapman, the Brontës, Whitman
—authors not precisely fashionable in the mid-nineteenth
century. He was alert also to what was best (and worst) in
his older and immediate contemporaries; but after 1879 he
not merely failed to respond to younger contemporaries,
he revoked some of his former generosities.

In the earlier criticism, he is sinuous in his sympathies. A
devoted classic, Swinburne found Shakespeare's *Troilus and
Cressida* repulsive; he acutely senses that all the characters
(with the possible exception of Ulysses) are flawed, even
though he tends to identify Thersites' point of view with
that of the author. Yet he can still refer to 'this . . . mysterious
and magnificent monster . . . one of the most admirable of
all Shakespeare's works' at a time when few nineteenth-
century critics could bring themselves even to discuss the
play. In *A Study of Shakespeare*, he takes a pioneering glance
at the earlier quarto of *Hamlet*. About multiple authorship
of the plays in the Shakespeare Folio, he is cautious: he finds
that *Henry VIII* is Shakespeare's absolutely and he refuses
to enlarge the canon to admit the agreeable, anonymous
Edward III, in a stylistic analysis of some length. His attacks
on the New Shakespeare Society and on the yet wilder
logic of certain German scholars are still funny and apposite.
Himself an inspired amateur, Swinburne tended to have a
low opinion of professional scholars. He knew as much, if
not more than they, and the poetry was the thing. The

oddity of his prose style often veils a luminous common sense about literary matters.

His dramatic criticism, is, however, less rewarding than his earlier essays on art and literature. The 'Notes on Designs of the Old Masters at Florence' and the 'Notes on the Royal Academy Exhibition of 1868' with their lingering cadences and troubled images influenced Pater (though Rossetti's prose is the archetype). Such evocations of works of art belong to a tradition of 'impressionist' criticism which includes the æsthete and poisoner T. G. Wainewright, Hazlitt and Gautier. In this tradition, impressions could be both subject and æsthetic object simultaneously. If we compare Swinburne's evocations of particular artefacts with those of Pater, we discover that, while both remain eloquent and suggestive, Pater more frequently intuits elements in the picture or the sculpture apparently not available from the historical record or within the limits of the observer's temperament.

Of the literary essays, we may note that on *Les Fleurs du Mal*, contributed in 1862 to the *Spectator*, in which Swinburne recognizes that 'those who will look for them may find moralities in plenty behind every poem of M. Baudelaire'. But in what is a very early though not simple-minded statement of the 'Art for Art's Sake' position in England, he urges that it is not the business of art to teach *directly*. If an artist is scrupulous in matters of art, his work will involve a corresponding moral scrupulousness. The *William Blake* essay contains the mature exposition of Swinburne's 'Art for Art's sake' views. We may conclude with this quotation: 'Art is not like fire or water, a good servant and a bad master; rather the reverse . . . Handmaid of religion, exponent of duty, servant of fact, pioneer of morality, she cannot in any way become . . . Her business is not to do good on other grounds, but do good on her own: all is well with her while she sticks fast to that.'

Swinburne's essay on Byron begins by praising the third and fourth cantos of *Childe Harolde*, but then sharply insists that the great Byron is only to be found in the satires, broadly the modern view. The polemical 'Notes on *Poems and Ballads*' and 'Under the Microscope', Swinburne's contribution to the 'Fleshly School' controversy of 1872', are written in the avowedly biased tradition of the pamphlet and still make trenchant reading.

His *William Blake* is not merely essential for an understanding of Swinburne's work in the 1860s, it remains one of the major documents of nineteenth-century criticism. An intensely difficult author is sympathetically and intelligently handled. Swinburne dismisses at once the widely held contemporary opinion that the obscurity of Blake's writing and the eccentricity of his opinions originate in his madness. Introducing a commentary on the Prophetic Books, Swinburne did not succeed, perhaps hardly wished to, in uncovering their dark mythological scheme. He was handicapped also by not being aware of the *Four Zoas*, which would have provided something of a key. But he does analyse searchingly such a work as *The Marriage of Heaven and Hell*, which he considered to be Blake's greatest. The heart of the volume, however, lies in the first two sections: the 'Life and Designs' and the 'Lyrical Poems'. His Blake is of course made in Swinburne's image; as Harold Bloom puts it: 'an uneasy blend of Rousseau and De Sade, at once somehow an heroic naturalist and an erotic rebel straining against even the limits of nature in his vitalism'. Swinburne seizes on any opportunity to stress pagan joy in Blake and recounts the oral report that Blake had suggested the introduction of a second wife into his household. Failure to grasp that, for Blake, nature and imagination were antithetical, lies at the heart of Swinburne's fruitful misunderstanding of Blake. For Swinburne anti-natural was generally limited to anti-conventional. Morality for him remains polarized with Art for Art's sake, there is no middle view, no alternative. As one critic observes, he is 'hamstrung by the very puritan tradition he is trying to shake off'. Consequently, he anticipates Yeats in making a gnostic of Blake, a sexual (but not ascetic) antinomian, for whom the erotic is demonic illusion. The demiurge who 'created the sexual and separate body of man did but cleave in twain "the divine humanity" which without price and without covenant and without law . . . is a divine demon, liable to error, subduable by and through the very created nature of his invention, which he for the present imprisons and torments. *His* law is the law of Moses, which according to the Manichean heresy Christ came to reverse as diabolic.' It is perhaps less that Swinburne misunderstands, than that he diminishes Blake by imprisoning him in this simple dualism of preference for desire and energy over reason and restraint. *The Marriage of Heaven and Hell* Swinburne brilliantly but falsely interprets as an inversion of accepted values, not sensing that the 'spiralling contraries' of that *mélange* of prose and verse are both necessary. Missing the two meanings of 'Hell' in 'The Marriage', he actually invents two meanings of 'nature' in *Jerusalem* and *Milton* because his neo-Sadian theology requires that. Wonderful book though it is, the *William Blake* could have been a different, perhaps better work if Swinburne had not as usual paused at the point of moving beyond a Blake necessary for himself. He recognizes, for example, that the *Songs of Innocence and of Experience* are counterpointed, but does not proceed with the insight; and after one piece of actual exegesis of the Prophetic Books which scholars accept as correct, Swinburne hastily flinches 'Lest, however, we be found unawares on the side of those hapless angels and baboons, we will abstain with all due care from any not indispensable analysis,' yet what Yeats was to term 'the great procession of symbols' was surely indispensable.

X

Swinburne was a pertinacious author of poetic dramas. For this activity, the nineteenth century was barely auspicious. To isolate any single cause is difficult: there was the Evangelical assault on the play and the player; the tyranny of Shakespeare, while English prose drama was itself in eclipse (painfully recovering in the 1860s with the work of Taylor and Robertson). The English scene, moreover, had been unusually barren of good dramatic criticism. Although there were actor-managers ready to encourage poets, Tennyson and Browning achieved no more than moderate success. However, Shelley and Beddoes who wrote for private reading rather than performance, were more successful—could at least challenge the later Jacobeans. Swinburne follows their practice (we noted how in his own dramatic criticism he took little account of stage conditions).

His two early plays *The Queen-Mother* and *Rosamond* reveal Jacobean influence crossed with Pre-Raphaelitism. In either case, a strong matriarch, Queens Catharine and Eleanor, destroy other women. The character of Denise, maid-in-waiting and devoted mistress to Henry III of France, is a triumph. The play pivots on her role as Queen's pawn in bringing on the King's involvement with the Bartholomew massacre and her reactions on realizing she has been misled. *Chastelard*, first of the Mary Stuart trilogy, is closely tuned with *Poems and Ballads*. Mary at once enjoys and detests her role as Fatal Woman; Chastelard himself is one who finds erotic consummation in death, but it is difficult for the reader to involve his emotions with either. The exposition is competent, the verse often striking and the scene where Chastelard induces Mary to kiss him on the neck at the spot where he knows the axe will fall is luridly memorable. In *Bothwell* and *Mary Stuart*, Swinburne perceptibly becomes more constrained by historical sources and more sympathetic to Mary but in these plays her character is comparatively weakly projected. The later plays sometimes display routine skill in exploiting situation; but few of them now hold their interest. *The Sisters* (1892), however, has unusual qualities. Set ostensibly in 1815, it involves once more the close aristocratic world of *Love's*

Cross Currents and is deeply autobiographical—the last reworking of the Mary Gordon story. The blank verse is relaxed:

Anne:　　April again, and not a word of war
　　　　　Last year, and not a year ago, it was
　　　　　That we sat wondering when good news would come.

Mabel:　　And had not heard or learnt in lesson books
　　　　　If such a place there was as Waterloo.

　　　　　　...

Reginald:　We are lucky. There's the old laboratory made
　　　　　It seems for our stage purpose, where you know
　　　　　Sir Edward kept his chemicals and things—
　　　　　Collections of the uncanniest odds and ends

That last epithet has a casual 1890s note. Swinburne should have realized that his general idiom was suitable for comedy or tragi-farce, but not for tragedy. Anne, the jealous, murdering sister, deviates into high blank verse and the play reaches a faltering climax through a holocaust which, although set in a nineteenth-century drawing room, is worthy of Jacobean tragedy.

XI

Swinburne discovered his poetic identity through the distinction between personality and 'self' trapped within personality, in his case an absurd body, without access to women. His solution was to transmute concrete being into artifice by imitation, parody, and caricature. In other words he tried to release identity by remoulding the styles of the past into an integrity that was of the surface only, and thus to achieve selfhood with the aid of tradition (see p. 19). But the price was negation of development; the quest for 'unity of being' was broken off at a stage of precarious balance. This disequilibrium begins with *Songs before Sunrise* where the 'self' is unlocated, is operatically merely 'voice'. Such failure of the redemptive imagination in 'the middle years' has precedents in romantic poetry; in, for example, Wordsworth and Coleridge, though both these poets were able to transfer loss into triumph. But Wordsworth, however unlike Swinburne in most respects, furnishes a model of genius mutating into low-keyed talent. Swinburne found no means of living out a mythology, or rather the self-mythology he could live by proved self-defeating. As a consequence Swinburne was not able to take up history and nation into the self-drama. He belonged to a dying class; there was no idea or group with which he could fruitfully identify and this explains the abstractions and inconsistencies of his political attitudes. The price of negating development was that his work finally became pure surface over void. Those strict forms of rondeau and sonnet by which he sought to chasten an imagined abundance merely emphasized poverty. Fixed at the level of tension between 'personality' and 'self', Swinburne failed to arrive at a notion of anti-self 'filling up all that the self fell short in'. As a consequence the self was never re-born. Had Swinburne correctly read *The Marriage of Heaven and Hell*, he would have grasped that the dialectic of poetic development lay through 'spiralling contraries'.

ALGERNON CHARLES SWINBURNE

A Select Bibliography

(Place of publication London, unless stated otherwise)

Bibliography:

A BIBLIOGRAPHY OF THE WRITINGS IN PROSE AND VERSE OF A. C. SWINBURNE, by T. J. Wise, 2 vols (1919–1920).

THE ASHLEY LIBRARY: A Catalogue of printed books, manuscripts and autograph letters, collected by T. J. Wise, 11 vols (1922–36)
—Vols VI-X, 1925-30, contain Swinburne entries.

A SWINBURNE LIBRARY, by T. J. Wise (1925)
—a reprint of Vol. VI; privately printed; limited edition.

SWINBURNE'S LITERARY CAREER AND FAME, by C. J. Hyder; Durham, N. C. (1933).

AN ENQUIRY INTO THE NATURE OF CERTAIN NINETEENTH-CENTURY PAMPHLETS, by J. Carter and H. G. Pollard (1934)
—exposes Wise's forgeries of editions of Swinburne.

BIBLIOGRAPHIES OF TWELVE VICTORIAN AUTHORS, by T. G. Ehrsam, R. H. Deily and R. M. Smith; New York (1936).

FORGING AHEAD, by W. Partington; New York (1939)
—enlarged ed., under the title *Thomas J. Wise in the Original Cloth*, London, 1946.

THE FIRM OF CHARLES OTTLEY, LANDON & CO.: Footnote to An Enquiry, by J. Carter and H. G. Pollard (1948).

THE VICTORIAN POETS: A Guide to Research, ed. F. E. Faverty, Cambridge, Mass. (1956)
—revised edition, 1968. Swinburne studies are discussed by C. K. Hyder.

'Swinburne Manuscripts at Texas', by W. B. Todd, *Texas Quarterly*, II, Autumn 1959.

THOMAS J. WISE CENTENARY STUDIES, ed. W. B. Todd; Austin (1959)
—essays, by J. Carter, H. G. Pollard, W. B. Todd.

PRE-RAPHAELITISM: A Bibliocritical Study, by W. E. Fredeman; Cambridge, Mass. (1965).

Collected Works:

THE POETICAL WORKS; New York (1884)
—also includes some dramas: *The Queen-Mother, Rosamond, Chastelard, Atalanta in Calydon, Bothwell* and *Erechtheus.*

THE POEMS, 6 vols (1904).

THE TRAGEDIES, 5 vols (1905).

POEMS AND TRAGEDIES, 2 vols; Philadelphia (1910).

THE GOLDEN PINE EDITION, 7 vols (1917–25).

COLLECTED POETICAL WORKS, 2 vols (1924).

THE COMPLETE WORKS, 20 vols (1925–7)

—the Bonchurch Edition; Vols I–X contain the Poetry and Dramas.

THE SWINBURNE LETTERS, ed. C. Y. Lang, 6 vols; New Haven (1959–62).

Selected Works:

SELECTIONS, ed. R. H. Stoddard; New York (1884).

SELECTIONS (1887).

LYRICAL POEMS, ed. W. Sharp; Leipzig (1901)

—the Tauchnitz edition.

DEAD LOVE AND OTHER INEDITED PIECES; Portland, Maine (1901).

SELECTED POEMS, ed. W. M. Payne; Boston (1905).

SELECTED LYRICAL POEMS; New York (1906).

POEMS, ed. A. Beatty; New York (1906).

DRAMAS, selected and edited by A. Beatty; New York (1909).

A PILGRIMAGE OF PLEASURE, ESSAYS AND STUDIES; Boston (1913)

—contains *A Pilgrimage of Pleasure, Dead Love, Les Fleurs du Mal, Charles Dickens* and some reviews; also includes a Bibliography of the works of Swinburne, by E. J. O'Brien.

THE SPRINGTIDE OF LIFE: Poems of Childhood, ed. E. Gosse (1918).

POEMS, ed. E. Rhys; New York (1919)

—Modern Library edition.

SELECTIONS, ed. E. Gosse and T. J. Wise (1919).

A GOLDEN BOOK OF SWINBURNE'S LYRICS, ed. E. H. Blakeney (1922).

THE TRIUMPH OF TIME AND OTHER POEMS, ed. G. S. Viereck; Girard, Kansas (1925).

SELECTIONS, ed. W. O. Raymond; New York (1925).

SELECTIONS, ed. H. M. Burton; Cambridge (1927).

SELECTED POEMS, ed. H. Wolfe (1928).

THE BEST OF SWINBURNE, ed. C. K. Hyder and L. Chase; New York (1937).

SELECTED POEMS, ed. L. Binyon (1939)

—World's Classics edition.

POEMS AND PROSE, ed. R. Church (1940)

—Everyman Library edition.

SELECTED POEMS, ed. H. Treece (1948).

SELECTED POEMS, ed. H. Hare (1950).

SELECTED POEMS, ed. E. Shanks (1950).

A SWINBURNE ANTHOLOGY: Verse, Drama, Prose, Criticism, ed. K. Foss (1955).

SWINBURNE: a Selection, ed. E. Sitwell (1960).

POEMS, ed. B. Dobrée (1961).

SELECTED POETRY AND PROSE, ed. J. D. Rosenberg; New York (1968).

POEMS AND BALLADS AND ATALANTA IN CALYDON, ed. M. Peckham; New York (1970).

Separate Works:

'Willam Congreve', in IMPERIAL DICTIONARY OF UNIVERSAL BIOGRAPHY, ed. J. F. Waller, 3 vols (1857)

—reprinted in *Pericles and Other Studies*, 1914.

THE QUEEN-MOTHER; ROSAMOND: Two Plays (1860).

'Dead Love', *Once a Week*, October 1862. *Short Story*

—reprinted in about 1888 in a forged first edition dated 1864; facsimile, 1904.

'The Sundew', *The Spectator*, 26 July 1862

—a revised version appears in *Poems and Ballads*, 1866.

'The Pilgrimage of Pleasure', In CHILDREN OF THE CHAPEL by Mary Gordon (1864)

—a Morality Play included as ch. v.

ATALANTA IN CALYDON: A Tragedy (1865)

—reprinted in facsimile, Oxford, 1930.

CHASTELARD: A Tragedy (1865).

POEMS AND BALLADS (1866)

—issued first by Moxon and then by Hotten.

NOTES ON POEMS AND REVIEWS (1866)

—Swinburne's reply to his critics; reprinted in *Swinburne Replies*, ed C. K. Hyder, Syracuse, 1966.

'Preface', in A SELECTION FROM THE WORKS OF LORD BYRON (1866)

—an excellent essay on Byron.

'Cleopatra', *The Cornhill Magazine*, September 1866

—a poem written to illustrate a drawing by F. Sandys. It was reprinted in about 1887 in a forged edition dated 1866.

AN APPEAL TO ENGLAND (1867). *Verse*

—for clemency to the Fenian rebels, published simultaneously in *The Morning Star* of 22 November and as a broadside.

'Regret', *The Fortnightly Review*, September 1867. *Verse*

—reprinted in revised form in *Poems and Ballads*, second series, 1878.

A SONG OF ITALY (1867).

WILLIAM BLAKE: A Critical essay (1868)
—the book seems to have been available in December 1867.

NOTES ON THE ROYAL ACADEMY EXHIBITION, 1868 (1868)
—reprinted with omissions in *Essays and Studies*, 1875.

'Siena', *Lippincott's Magazine*, June 1868
—separately printed the same year in Philadelphia and London.

'Introduction' in CHRISTABEL AND THE LYRICAL AND IMAGINATIVE POEMS OF S. T. COLERIDGE (1869).

ODE ON THE PROCLAMATION OF THE FRENCH REPUBLIC (1870).

'Tristram and Iseult: Prelude of an Unfinished Poem'. in PLEASURE: A HOLIDAY BOOK OF PROSE AND VERSE, [ed. J. Friswell] (1871)
—revised in *Tristram of Lyonesse*, 1882.

SONGS BEFORE SUNRISE (1871).

BOTHWELL, ACT ONE (1871)
—privately printed.

UNDER THE MICROSCOPE (1872)
—a masterfully ironic prose pamphlet directed against the philistine critics of Rossetti and himself.

LE TOMBEAU DE THÉOPHILE GAUTIER [ed. A. Lemerre]; Paris (1873)
—poems by various authors on the death of Gautier; poems by Swinburne are in four languages, two in English, two in French, one in Latin and one in Greek.

BOTHWELL: A Tragedy (1874).

'Introduction' in THE WORKS OF GEORGE CHAPMAN (1874-5)
—also separately printed the same year.

SONGS OF TWO NATIONS (1875).

'The Devil's Due', *The Examiner*, 11 December 1875
—published under the pseudonym 'Thomas Maitland'. A privately printed edition, dated 1875, appeared about 1896 and is probably forged.

ESSAYS AND STUDIES (1875).

'Francis Beaumont'; 'John Fletcher' in ENCYCLOPAEDIA BRITANNICA (1875).

NOTE OF AN ENGLISH REPUBLICAN ON THE MUSCOVITE CRUSADE (1876).

'Introduction' in JOSEPH AND HIS BRETHREN: A Dramatic poem, by C. J. Wells (1876)
—I have suspected that Swinburne may have been more actively concerned with the revise.

ERECHTHEUS: A Tragedy (1876).

LESBIA BRANDON (1877). *Novel*

—only galley proofs printed, used by R. Hughes in his edition, 1952.

A NOTE ON CHARLOTTE BRONTË (1877).

'William Congreve' in ENCYCLOPAEDIA BRITANNICA (1877).

POEMS AND BALLADS: Second Series (1878).

AN ELECTION (1879). *Verse*

—a lithographed pamphlet.

'Frank Fane: a ballad', *The Pearl*, I, 1879

—an unsigned contribution to an 'underground' magazine.

SONGS OF THE SPRINGTIDES (1880).

SPECIMENS OF MODERN POETS: The Heptalogia, or, The Seven Against
Sense (1880)

—a volume of parodies.

STUDIES IN SONG (1880).

A STUDY OF SHAKESPEARE (1880).

MARY STUART: A Tragedy (1881).

TRISTRAM OF LYONESSE AND OTHER POEMS (1882).

A CENTURY OF ROUNDELS (1883)

—the strict form, adopted by Swinburne to chasten his fluency;
the object was not achieved.

'Dolorida' in WALNUTS AND WINE, ed. A. Moore (1883).

—verses in French.

'Introduction' in LES CENCI; Paris (1883)

—introduction in French to T. Dorian's translation of Shelley's play.

'Christopher Marlowe' in ENCYLOPAEDIA BRITANNICA (1883).

'Mary Queen of Scots' in ENCYCLOPAEDIA BRITANNICA (1883).

'Wordsworth and Byron', *The Nineteenth Century*, April-May 1884.

A MIDSUMMER HOLIDAY AND OTHER POEMS (1884).

MARINO FALIERO: A Tragedy (1885).

THE COMMONWEAL: A Song for Unionists (1886)

—reprinted from *The Times*, 1 July 1886.

MISCELLANIES (1886)

—a collection of previously printed periodical and encyclopaedia
articles.

A STUDY OF VICTOR HUGO (1886).

'Introduction' in THOMAS MIDDLETON, ed. H. Ellis (1887)

—the Mermaid edition.

A WORD FOR THE NAVY (1887). *Verse*

—privately printed.

THE WHIPPINGHAM PAPERS (1888)
—privately printed; about half the volume was written by Swinburne.

'Cyril Tourneur' in ENCYCLOPAEDIA BRITANNICA (1889).

A STUDY OF BEN JONSON (1889).

POEMS AND BALLADS: Third Series (1889)

THE BALLAD OF DEAD MEN'S BAY (1889).

'A Logical Ballad of Home Rule', *St James's Gazette*, 2 March 1889.

A SEQUENCE OF SONNETS ON THE DEATH OF ROBERT BROWNING (1890)
—privately printed.

'Preface' in THE HESPERIDES AND NOBLE NUMBERS, by R. Herrick (1891)
—the Muses' Library edition.

MUSIC: An Ode (1892).

THE SISTERS: A Tragedy (1892).

GRACE DARLING (1893). *Verse*
—privately printed.

ASTROPHEL AND OTHER POEMS (1894).

STUDIES IN PROSE AND POETRY (1894).

ROBERT BURNS: A Poem; Edinburgh (1896)
—privately printed and pirated.

THE TALE OF BALEN (1896). *Verse*.

'Introduction' to AURORA LEIGH, by E. B. Browning (1898)

A CHANNEL PASSAGE (1899).

ROSAMOND, QUEEN OF THE LOMBARDS: A Tragedy (1899).

'Victor Hugo' in the ENCYCLOPAEDIA BRITANNICA (1902).

PERCY BYSSHE SHELLEY; Philadelphia (1903)
—also published in *Chambers Cyclopaedia of English Literature*, 1903.

A CHANNEL PASSAGE AND OTHER POEMS (1904)
—includes numerous poems previously only published in periodicals.

LOVE'S CROSS CURRENTS: A Year's Letters (1905). *Novel*
—first published by instalments in *The Tatler*, 25 August—29 December 1877. Pirated in an edition from Portland, Maine, 1901 and published in a fuller version in 1905.

'Introduction' to PERICLES (1907)
—Vol. XIII of Lee's edition of Shakespeare, 1906–9.

THE DUKE OF GANDIA (1908). *Drama*
—this reads like an early work.

THE AGE OF SHAKESPEARE (1908).

M. PRUDHOMME AT THE INTERNATIONAL EXHIBITION (1909)
—privately printed.

OF LIBERTY AND LOYALTY (1909)
—privately printed.

THE SAVIOUR OF SOCIETY (1909). *Verse*
—privately printed.

THE PORTRAIT (1909). *Verse*
—privately printed.

THE MARRIAGE OF MONNA LISA (1909)
—privately printed.

THE CHRONICLE OF QUEEN FREDEGOND (1909)
—privately printed.

IN THE TWILIGHT: A Poem (1909)
—privately printed.

LORD SCALES: A Ballad by a Borderer (1909)
—privately printed.

LORD SOULIS: A Ballad by a Borderer (1909)
—privately printed.

BURD MARGARET: A Ballad by a Borderer (1909)
—privately printed.

THE WORM OF SPINDLESTONHEUGH: A Ballad by a Borderer (1909)
—privately printed.

BORDER BALLADS (1909)
—privately printed. Contains 'Earl Robert', 'Duriesdyke', 'Westland Well'.

ODE TO MAZZINI (1909)
—privately printed.

SHAKESPEARE (1909).

A CRIMINAL CASE: A sketch (1910)
—privately printed.

A RECORD OF FRIENDSHIP (1910)
—privately printed; Swinburne's account of his relationship with Rossetti and Lizzie Rossetti written in 1882 after Rossetti's death.

THE BALLADE OF TRUTHFUL CHARLES AND OTHER POEMS (1910)
—privately printed.

LES FLEURS DU MAL, AND OTHER STUDIES (1913)
—privately printed.

CHARLES DICKENS (1913)
—reprinted in part from *The Quarterly Review*, July 1902.

A STUDY OF VICTOR HUGO'S 'LES MISÉRABLES', ed. E. Gosse (1914)
—privately printed; the first and fifth essays are not by Swinburne.

PERICLES AND OTHER STUDIES (1914)
—privately printed. Reprints *Pericles* with essays and articles not separately published elsewhere.

THOMAS NABBES: A critical monograph (1914)
—privately printed.

CHRISTOPHER MARLOWE IN RELATION TO GREENE, PEELE AND LODGE (1914)
—privately printed.

THÉOPHILE, ed. E. Gosse (1915)
—privately printed.

LADY MAISIE'S BAIRN, AND OTHER POEMS (1915)
—privately printed.

POEMS FROM VILLON, AND OTHER FRAGMENTS (1916)
—privately printed.

THE DEATH OF SIR JOHN FRANKLIN (1916)
—privately printed. An undergraduate poem.

THE TRIUMPH OF GLORIANA, ed. E. Gosse (1916)
—privately printed.

POETICAL FRAGMENTS (1916)
—privately printed.

A VISION OF BAGS, ed. E. Gosse (1916). *Burlesque*
—privately printed.

WEARIESWA': A Ballad (1917)
—privately printed.

THE POSTHUMOUS POEMS, ed. E. Gosse and T. J. Wise (1917).

RONDEAUX PARISIENS (1917)
—privately printed.

THE ITALIAN MOTHER, AND OTHER POEMS (1918)
—privately printed.

THE RIDE FROM MILAN, AND OTHER POEMS (1918)
—privately printed.

THE TWO KNIGHTS, AND OTHER POEMS (1918)
—privately printed.

A LAY OF LILIES, AND OTHER POEMS (1918)
—privately printed.

QUEEN YSEULT: A Poem in six cantos (1918)
—privately printed.

UNDERGRADUATE SONNETS (1918)
—privately printed.

LANCELOT, THE DEATH OF RUDEL, AND OTHER POEMS (1918)
—privately printed.

THE CHARACTER AND OPINIONS OF DR JOHNSON (1918)
—privately printed.

CONTEMPORARIES OF SHAKESPEARE, ed. E. Gosse and T. J. Wise (1919).

THE QUEEN'S TRAGEDY (1919)
—privately printed.

FRENCH LYRICS (1919)
—privately printed.

BALLADS OF THE ENGLISH BORDER, ed. W. A. MacInnes (1925)
—includes all known previously published and unpublished ballads.

SWINBURNE'S HYPERION, AND OTHER POEMS, ed. G. Lafourcade (1928).

LUCRETIA BORGIA: The Chronicle of Tebaldeo Tebaldei, ed. R. Hughes (1942).

SWINBURNE: 'CHANGES OF ASPECT' AND 'SHORT NOTES', ed. C. K. Hyder, *Publications of the Modern Language Association, LVIII*, March 1943.

A ROUNDEL OF RETREAT; [Washington, DC 1950]
—privately printed; the imprint, clearly a joke, reads: London, Charles Ottley, Landon & Co., 1950.

PASIPHAË: A Poem, ed. R. Hughes (1950)
—an extremely interesting fragment dated approximately 1866.

WILL DREW AND PHIL CREWE AND FRANK FANE BY A GREAT ENGLISH LITERARY FIGURE [1962?]
—privately printed.

LE PRINCE PROLÉTAIRE; Bethesda, Maryland (1963)
—privately printed.

THE INFLUENCE OF THE ROMAN CENSORSHIP ON THE MORALS OF THE PEOPLE; Brooklyn (1964)
—privately printed.

NEW WRITINGS BY SWINBURNE, ed. C. Y. Lang; Syracuse, NY (1964)
—the contents include some uncollected poems, the early burlesques, *La Soeur de la Reine* and *La fille du Policeman*, with extensive annotations.

SWINBURNE REPLIES, ed. C. K. Hyder; Syracuse, NY (1966)
—reprints *Notes on Poems and Reviews, Under the Microscope* and the *Dedicating Epistle to the Collection of 1899* with an introduction and notes.

Some Biographical and Critical Studies:

'Swinburne's *Atalanta in Calydon*', by Baron Houghton [R. M. Milnes], *Edinburgh Review*, CXXII, 249, July 1865.

'Mr Swinburne's *Chastelard*', by Baron Houghton [R. M. Milnes], *The Fortnightly Review*, IV, 23, 15 April 1866.

Review of *Poems and Ballads*, by R. W. Buchanan, *Athenaeum*, II, 1866.

'Immorality in authorship' by R. W. Buchanan, *The Fortnightly Review*, VI, 33, 15 September 1866.

'Mr Swinburne's new poems' [by J. Morley], *Saturday Review*, XXII, 4 August 1866.

SWINBURNE'S POEMS AND BALLADS: A Criticism, by W. M. Rossetti (1866).

'The Swinburne controversy', by J. Thomson, *National Reformer*, 23 December 1866
—repeated in his *Satires and Profanities*, 1884.

Review of *William Blake*, by M. D. Conway, *The Fortnightly Review*, III n.s., 14, 1 February 1868.

'The Poetry of the Period: Mr Swinburne', by A. Austin, *Temple Bar*, XXVI, July 1869
—reprinted in his *The Poetry of the Period*, 1870.

THE FLESHLY SCHOOL OF POETRY, by R. W. Buchanan (1872).

'The latest development of literary poetry: Swinburne, Rossetti, Morris', by W. J. Courthorpe, *The Quarterly Review*, CXXXII, 263, January 1872.

'Cosmic emotion', by W. K. Clifford, *The Nineteenth Century*, II, October 1877
—repeated in his *Lectures and Essays*, 1879.

HISTOIRES INSOLITES, by Villiers de l'Isle Adam; Paris (1888)
—contains 'Le sadisme anglais'.

Review of *Poems and Ballads: third series*, by O. Wilde, *The Pall Mall Gazette*, 27 June 1889
—repeated in his *Reviews*, Vol. II, 1910.

MODERN STUDIES, by O. Elton (1907).

ALGERNON CHARLES SWINBURNE: A Critical Study, by E. Thomas (1912).

CATALOGUE OF THE LIBRARY OF SWINBURNE. Sotheby, Wilkinson and Hodge, 19–21 June 1916.

THE LIFE OF ALGERNON CHARLES SWINBURNE, by E. Gosse (1917)
—repeated in Bonchurch edition, Vol. XIX.

THE BOYHOOD OF SWINBURNE, by M. C. J. Leith (1917).

'Swinburne' by A. Symons, *The Fortnightly Review*, CI n.s., 605, May 1917.

'The first draft of Swinburne's "Anactoria"', by E. Gosse, *Modern Language Review*, XIV, July 1919.

—also privately printed, n.d.; repeated in *Aspects and Impressions*, 1922.

THE SACRED WOOD, by T. S. Eliot (1920)

—contains essays: 'Swinburne as critic'; 'Swinburne as poet'.

THE HOME LIFE OF SWINBURNE, by C. Watts-Dunton (1922).

'Swinburne et Baudelaire', by G. Lafourcade, *Revue Anglo-américaine*, I, February 1924.

'*Atalanta in Calydon*: le manuscrit, les sources', by G. Lafourcade, *Revue Anglo-americaine*, III, October-December, 1925.

A STUDY OF SWINBURNE, by T. E. Welby (1926).

SWINBURNE, by H. Nicolson (1926).

'Swinburne and Whitman', by G. Lafourcade, *Modern Language Review*, XXII, January 1927

—revised version, *Revue Anglo-americaine*, IX, October 1931.

LA JEUNESSE DE SWINBURNE, 1837–1867, by G. Lafourcade, 2 vols; Paris (1928).

'*Laus Veneris* and the Tannhäuser legend', by C. K. Hyder, *Publications of the Modern Language Association*, XLV, December 1930.

LA CARNE, LA MORTE E IL DIAVOLO NELLA LETTERATURA ROMANTICA, by M. Praz; Florence (1930)

—translated as *The Romantic Agony*, Oxford, 1933. A pathography of Romantic literature.

'The medieval background in "The Leper"', by C. K. Hyder, *Publications of the Modern Language Association*, XLVI, December 1931.

SWINBURNE'S LITERARY CAREER AND FAME, by C. K. Hyder, Durham, NC (1931).

SWINBURNE: A Literary Biography, by G. Lafourcade (1932).

'Swinburne and the popular ballad', by C. K. Hyder, *Publications of the Modern Language Association*, XLIX, March 1934.

'L'algolagnied e Swinburne', by G. Lafourcade, *Hippocrate*, March-April 1935.

'Le triomphe du temps: ou la réputation de Swinburne', by G. Lafourcade, *Études Anglaises*, I, March 1937.

'Swinburne's mature standards of criticism', by R. C. Child, *Publications of the Modern Language Association*, LII, September 1937.

'Unpublished Swinburne', by R. Hughes, *Life and Letters*, LVI, January 1948.

'Swinburne's loyalty to the House of Stuart', by C. Dahl, *Studies in Philology*, XLVI, July 1949.

'Robert Buchanan and the fleshly controversy', by J. A. Cassidy, *Publications of the Modern Language Association*, LXVII, March 1952.

'A neglected phase of the Aesthetic Movement: English Parnassianism', by J. K. Robinson, *Publications of the Modern Language Association*, LXVIII, September 1953
—relates Swinburne's experiments in Old French forms to similar work by Lang, Gosse, Dobson, etc.

SWINBURNE'S BOO, by J. S. Mayfield; Bethesda (1953)
—privately printed; repeated in *English Miscellany* (Rome), IV, 1953; separately bound and privately reissued, Washington DC, 1954.

'The first chorus of *Atalanta*', by C. Y. Lang, *Yale University Library Gazette*, XXVII, January 1953.

THE CRITIC'S ALCHEMY, by R. Z. Temple; New York (1953)
—on Swinburne as critic and interpreter of French literature.

'Some Swinburne Manuscripts', by C. Y. Lang, *Journal of Rutgers University Library*, XVIII, December 1954.

'A reconstructed Swinburne ballad', by A. W. Henry [Ehrenpreis], *Harvard Library Bulletin*, XII, Autumn 1958.

'The Fitzwilliam manuscript of Swinburne's *Atalanta*, verses 1,038–1,204', by P. R. Baum, *Modern Language Review*, LIV, 1959.

'*Atalanta* in manuscript', by C. Y. Lang, *Yale University Library Gazette*, XXXVII, July 1962.

SWINBURNE'S THEORY OF POETRY, by T. E. Connolly; Albany (1964).

THE CROWNS OF APOLLO: Swinburne's Principles of Literature and Art, by R. L. Peters; Detroit (1965).

'Swinburne', by J. D. Rosenberg, *Victorian Studies*, XI, ii, December 1967.

'A Rare Find', *American Book Collector*, XVII, 6 March 1967
—two missing pages of *Lesbia Brandon*.

'Swinburne's Poetry and Twentieth-Century Criticism', by R. E. Lougy, *Dalhousie Review*, XLVIII, Autumn 1968.

'The Structure of Swinburne's *Tristram of Lyonesse*,' by K. McSweeney, *Queen's Quarterly*, LXXV, iv, Winter 1968.

SWINBURNE: A Critical Biography, by J. O. Fuller (1968)
—useful, if somewhat highlighted.

'A. C. Swinburne's "Hymn to Proserpine": The Work Sheets', by
R. L. Peters, *Publications of the Modern Language Association*,
LXXXIII, October 1968.

SWINBURNE: The Critical Heritage, ed. C. K. Hyder (1970)
—a useful anthology of views of Swinburne's work and personality
up to the period before the First World War.

Victorian Poetry, IX, i–ii, Spring-Summer 1971
—a special issue devoted to Swinburne, edited by C. Y. Lang,
containing some of the finest criticism to date. Particularly useful
are essays by Thomas L. Wymar and Richard Mathews on *Atalanta;*
on 'Swinburne, Sade and Blake' by Julian Baird; on 'Anactoria'
by David A. Cook and Joseph J. McGann on 'Ave Atque Vale'.

SWINBURNE'S POETICS, by M. Raymond; The Hague (1971).

SWINBURNE: An Experiment in Criticism, by J. J. McGann; Chicago
(1972).

'Swinburne, Robert Buchanan, W. S. Gilbert', by W. D. Jenkins,
Studies in Philology, LXXIX, iii, 1972
—suggests that there are reflections of Swinburne's sado-masochism
in some of the choric passages in *Patience*, and relates Grosvenor to
Buchanan.

Manuscripts:

There are numerous manuscripts extant. Particularly important are
those in the Ashley collection in the British Museum.

WRITERS AND THEIR WORK

General Surveys:
THE DETECTIVE STORY IN BRITAIN:
Julian Symons
THE ENGLISH BIBLE: Donald Coggan
ENGLISH VERSE EPIGRAM:
G. Rostrevor Hamilton
ENGLISH HYMNS: A. Pollard
ENGLISH MARITIME WRITING:
Hakluyt to Cook: Oliver Warner
THE ENGLISH SHORT STORY I & II:
T. O. Beachcroft
THE ENGLISH SONNET: P. Cruttwell
ENGLISH SERMONS: Arthur Pollard
ENGLISH TRANSLATORS and
TRANSLATIONS: J. M. Cohen
ENGLISH TRAVELLERS IN THE
NEAR EAST: Robin Fedden
THREE WOMEN DIARISTS: M. Willy

Sixteenth Century and Earlier:
FRANCIS BACON: J. Max Patrick
BEAUMONT & FLETCHER: Ian Fletcher
CHAUCER: Nevill Coghill
GOWER & LYDGATE: Derek Pearsall
RICHARD HOOKER: A. Pollard
THOMAS KYD: Philip Edwards
LANGLAND: Nevill Coghill
LYLY & PEELE: G. K. Hunter
MALORY: M. C. Bradbrook
MARLOWE: Philip Henderson
SIR THOMAS MORE: E. E. Reynolds
RALEGH: Agnes Latham
SIDNEY: Kenneth Muir
SKELTON: Peter Green
SPENSER: Rosemary Freeman
THREE 14TH-CENTURY ENGLISH
MYSTICS: Phyllis Hodgson
TWO SCOTS CHAUCERIANS:
H. Harvey Wood
WYATT: Sergio Baldi

Seventeenth Century:
SIR THOMAS BROWNE: Peter Green
BUNYAN: Henri Talon
CAVALIER POETS: Robin Skelton
CONGREVE: Bonamy Dobrée
DONNE: F. Kermode
DRYDEN: Bonamy Dobrée
ENGLISH DIARISTS:
Evelyn and Pepys: M. Willy
FARQUHAR: A. J. Farmer
JOHN FORD: Clifford Leech
GEORGE HERBERT: T. S. Eliot
HERRICK: John Press
HOBBES: T. E. Jessop
BEN JONSON: J. B. Bamborough
LOCKE: Maurice Cranston
ANDREW MARVELL: John Press

MILTON: E. M. W. Tillyard
RESTORATION COURT POETS:
V. de S. Pinto
SHAKESPEARE: C. J. Sisson
CHRONICLES: Clifford Leech
EARLY COMEDIES: Derek Traversi
LATER COMEDIES: G. K. Hunter
FINAL PLAYS: F. Kermode
HISTORIES: L. C. Knights
POEMS: F. T. Prince
PROBLEM PLAYS: Peter Ure
ROMAN PLAYS: T. J. B. Spencer
GREAT TRAGEDIES: Kenneth Muir
THREE METAPHYSICAL POETS:
Margaret Willy
WEBSTER: Ian Scott-Kilvert
WYCHERLEY: P. F. Vernon

Eighteenth Century:
BERKELEY: T. E. Jessop
BLAKE: Kathleen Raine
BOSWELL: P. A. W. Collins
BURKE: T. E. Utley
BURNS: David Daiches
WM. COLLINS: Oswald Doughty
COWPER: N. Nicholson
CRABBE: R. L. Brett
DEFOE: J. R. Sutherland
FIELDING: John Butt
GAY: Oliver Warner
GIBBON: C. V. Wedgwood
GOLDSMITH: A. Norman Jeffares
GRAY: R. W. Ketton-Cremer
HUME: Montgomery Belgion
SAMUEL JOHNSON: S. C. Roberts
POPE: Ian Jack
RICHARDSON: R. F. Brissenden
SHERIDAN: W. A. Darlington
CHRISTOPHER SMART: G. Grigson
SMOLLETT: Laurence Brander
STEELE, ADDISON: A. R. Humphreys
STERNE: D. W. Jefferson
SWIFT: J. Middleton Murry
SIR JOHN VANBRUGH: Bernard Harris
HORACE WALPOLE: Hugh Honour

Nineteenth Century:
MATTHEW ARNOLD: Kenneth Allott
JANE AUSTEN: S. Townsend Warner
BAGEHOT: N. St John-Stevas
BRONTË SISTERS: Phyllis Bentley
BROWNING: John Bryson
E. B. BROWNING: Alethea Hayter
SAMUEL BUTLER: G. D. H. Cole
BYRON I, II & III: Bernard Blackstone
CARLYLE: David Gascoyne
LEWIS CARROLL: Derek Hudson
COLERIDGE: Kathleen Raine

CREEVEY & GREVILLE: J. Richardson
DE QUINCEY: Hugh Sykes Davies
DICKENS: K. J. Fielding
  EARLY NOVELS: T. Blount
  LATER NOVELS: B. Hardy
DISRAELI: Paul Bloomfield
GEORGE ELIOT: Lettice Cooper
FERRIER & GALT: W. M. Parker
FITZGERALD: Joanna Richardson
ELIZABETH GASKELL: Miriam Allott
GISSING: A. C. Ward
THOMAS HARDY: R. A. Scott-James
        and C. Day Lewis
HAZLITT: J. B. Priestley
HOOD: Laurence Brander
G. M. HOPKINS: Geoffrey Grigson
T. H. HUXLEY: William Irvine
KEATS: Edmund Blunden
LAMB: Edmund Blunden
LANDOR: G. Rostrevor Hamilton
EDWARD LEAR: Joanna Richardson
MACAULAY: G. R. Potter
MEREDITH: Phyllis Bartlett
JOHN STUART MILL: M. Cranston
WILLIAM MORRIS: P. Henderson
NEWMAN: J. M. Cameron
PATER: Ian Fletcher
PEACOCK: J. I. M. Stewart
ROSSETTI: Oswald Doughty
CHRISTINA ROSSETTI: G. Battiscombe
RUSKIN: Peter Quennell
SIR WALTER SCOTT: Ian Jack
SHELLEY: G. M. Matthews
SOUTHEY: Geoffrey Carnall
LESLIE STEPHEN: Phyllis Grosskurth
R. L. STEVENSON: G. B. Stern
SWINBURNE: H. J. C. Grierson
TENNYSON: B. C. Southam
THACKERAY: Laurence Brander
FRANCIS THOMPSON: P. Butter
TROLLOPE: Hugh Sykes Davies
OSCAR WILDE: James Laver
WORDSWORTH: Helen Darbishire

Twentieth Century:
CHINUA ACHEBE: A. Ravenscroft
W. H. AUDEN: Richard Hoggart
HILAIRE BELLOC: Renée Haynes
ARNOLD BENNETT: F. Swinnerton
EDMUND BLUNDEN: Alec M. Hardie
ROBERT BRIDGES: J. Sparrow
ANTHONY BURGESS: Carol M. Dix
ROY CAMPBELL: David Wright
JOYCE CARY: Walter Allen
G. K. CHESTERTON: C. Hollis
WINSTON CHURCHILL: John Connell
R. G. COLLINGWOOD: E. W. F. Tomlin
I. COMPTON-BURNETT:
        R. Glynn Grylls

JOSEPH CONRAD: Oliver Warner
WALTER DE LA MARE: K. Hopkins
NORMAN DOUGLAS: Ian Greenlees
LAWRENCE DURRELL: G. S. Fraser
T. S. ELIOT: M. C. Bradbrook
T. S. ELIOT: The Making of 'The Waste
       Land': M. C. Bradbrook
FIRBANK & BETJEMAN: J. Brooke
FORD MADOX FORD: Kenneth Young
E. M. FORSTER: Rex Warner
CHRISTOPHER FRY: Derek Stanford
JOHN GALSWORTHY: R. H. Mottram
ROBERT GRAVES: M. Seymour-Smith
GRAHAM GREENE: Francis Wyndham
L. P. HARTLEY: Paul Bloomfield
A. E. HOUSMAN: Ian Scott-Kilvert
TED HUGHES: Keith Sagar
ALDOUS HUXLEY: Jocelyn Brooke
HENRY JAMES: Michael Swan
PAMELA HANSFORD JOHNSON:
       Isabel Quigly
JAMES JOYCE: J. I. M. Stewart
RUDYARD KIPLING: Bonamy Dobrée
D. H. LAWRENCE: Kenneth Young
C. DAY LEWIS: Clifford Dyment
WYNDHAM LEWIS: E. W. F. Tomlin
COMPTON MACKENZIE: K. Young
LOUIS MACNEICE: John Press
KATHERINE MANSFIELD: Ian Gordon
JOHN MASEFIELD: L. A. G. Strong
SOMERSET MAUGHAM: J. Brophy
GEORGE MOORE: A. Norman Jeffares
J. MIDDLETON MURRY: Philip Mairet
R. K. NARAYAN: William Walsh
SEAN O'CASEY: W. A. Armstrong
GEORGE ORWELL: Tom Hopkinson
JOHN OSBORNE: Simon Trussler
HAROLD PINTER: John Russell Taylor
POETS OF 1939-45 WAR: R. N. Currey
ANTHONY POWELL: Bernard Bergonzi
POWYS BROTHERS: R. C. Churchill
J. B. PRIESTLEY: Ivor Brown
HERBERT READ: Francis Berry
FOUR REALIST NOVELISTS: V. Brome
BERNARD SHAW: A. C. Ward
EDITH SITWELL: John Lehmann
KENNETH SLESSOR: C. Semmler
C. P. SNOW: William Cooper
SYNGE & LADY GREGORY: E. Coxhead
DYLAN THOMAS: G. S. Fraser
G. M. TREVELYAN: J. H. Plumb
WAR POETS: 1914-18: E. Blunden
EVELYN WAUGH: Christopher Hollis
H. G. WELLS: Montgomery Belgion
PATRICK WHITE: R. F. Brissenden
ANGUS WILSON: K. W. Gransden
VIRGINIA WOOLF: B. Blackstone
W. B. YEATS: G. S. Fraser